The Optimistic Alien

FIGHTING BACK IN RISKY MARKETS

J. Michael Willard

The Optimistic Alien
Fighting Back in Risky Markets

ISBN-13: 978-1975608194
ISBN-10: 1975608194
Second Edition, May 2011

Published by VIDALIA HOUSE

www.vidaliahouse.com

©2010 J. Michael Willard

All rights reserved. No part of this publication may be reproduced, stored in a retrieval system ok transmitted in any form by any means, electronic, mechanical, photocopying, recording or otherwise, except brief extras for the purpose of review, without the express permission of the publisher and copyright owner.

Vidalia House and the Vidalia House logo are trademarks of Vidalia House and may not be used without written permission.

Chapters:

Introduction and Dedication
Chapter 1:   Why Are We Here?
Chapter 2:   Goodbye to Mountain Mama
Chapter 3:   Landing the Fish
Chapter 4:   Moscow Purgatory
Chapter 5:   A Confederacy of the Well-Intentioned
Chapter 6:   My Kingdom
Chapter 7:   A Place Apart
Chapter 8:   The Stealth Office
Chapter 9:   Moscow Bound
Chapter 10:   Then, The Other Shoe Dropped
Chapter 11:   Beginning Anew
Chapter 12:   Spreading Our Wings
Chapter 13:   A Way of Doing Business
Chapter 14:   Time Is Not A Renewable Resource And Other Sorrows
Chapter 15:   The Phoenix Rises – Again
Chapter 16:   Mistakes, I've Made a Few, But Then Again...
Chapter 17:   Survival of the Fittest
Chapter 18:   Revival of the Fittest
Chapter 19:   Battling the Giants
Chapter 20:   Up From the Crucible
Chapter 21:   Making the Tough Decisions
Chapter 22:   Where Are We Headed?
Chapter 23:   The Optimistic Alien: The Next (Not Last) Chapter
Postscript

Introduction and Dedication

This book can best be described as a confessional, perhaps not on the level of the 18th Century Jean Jacque Rousseau's famous work on confessions, but a pretty unvarnished picture of my more than a decade and a half in Eastern Europe.

It is also about a small company's struggle to survive against the odds in a harsh business climate, made worse by a huge communication conglomerate's efforts to put our company, Willard, out of business.

It is my intention not to be the star of this work, but merely a character actor, doing my best to hold on to my own lines and to deliver them as effectively as I know how. With this in mind, there are stars, for this book pays homage to a people, the Ukrainian people, and, I quickly add, a few Russians, Turks, Americans and one Estonian.

There are some passages as this book goes to press that I wondered if were necessary, for they appeal to my more basic instincts, that lowest common denominator where most of us at various times tread water. However, in the writing there was certainly no motivation for retribution. In the end, these chunks of verbiage, for the most part, stayed. If a few lines offend some, this was not my intention but merely represent collateral damage.

You will notice that I didn't list governments as part of my homage. Though made up of people, governments rarely represent the people in this area of the world. They merely serve as agents for other people with money. If one uses a chess analogy, government officials – all levels of government – are pawns parading as bishops. They have a certain flexibility of movement, but are certainly governed by higher ups. However, this is not a political book, though for necessary contexts it is important to bring up a few political moments. If any politician appears, it is a cameo and nothing more.

The Optimistic Alien is, at a minimum, a simple chronicle of the times. That, in itself I believe, will have you ask, "Did it really happen that way?" for they have been, indeed, interesting times, exciting times as a new nation was being born. But to "push the envelope – as the cliché goes (in advertising we call it "romancing the product") – this narrative is a social commentary on people, places and things as seen through the eyes of one who has lived through and reported on various revolutions, political and corporate wars and on the hum-drum that makes up the metronome life beat that is Eastern Europe.

Since this book takes up with the yellow leaf portion of my life, beginning on a hot but rainy August night in 1994 when I thought I was about to be fired from a job, I merely touch on episodes committed to an earlier book, *The Flak*. I have tried not to be repetitious to those who read the earlier work in its original English, or later in Russian as *PRschik*.

The fact is I have been on the periphery and in the middle of three revolutions, the latest being the bloodless Orange Revolution in Ukraine in 2005, and one war. Along the way, I have been given incredible opportunities to watch history in the making up close. I have met with kings and queens, prime ministers and famous legislative leaders, as well as singers, actors, and other entertainment stars. I would call them all my close personal friends, but they were not. They were generally handshake acquaintances while I was in the service of the momentarily famous.

However, there were genuine friends like Tex Ritter and Roy Acuff, fallen country stars of yesteryear; brush-by acquaintances such as John Thomas Scopes, of the so-called Scopes Monkey Trial; truly despicable characters such as James Earl Ray, the assassin of Dr. Martin Luther King Jr., and interesting but largely misunderstood folk like Dr. King's eldest son, Martin III, with whom on several occasions I shared fried chicken and Coca-Cola on my boat The *Kelly Dawn*.

The book takes you on my personal second chance career that has found me either in Kyiv, Ukraine or Moscow, Russia from that 1994 date until the present. I came to Ukraine at an age where many are eyeing retirement, a state of existence I do not even hope to dream about with five children, ranging in age from nine to 40 plus.

Though this book is presented chronologically, I address five Big Daddy challenges with which I – actually we – have had to deal and to overcome. Four were business and one personal – from which, perhaps, there are lessons to be taken. This includes: 1) Helping bring market reform to Ukraine; 2) Reinventing myself as an entrepreneur in Eastern Europe; 3) Fighting against a huge multinational that was trying to put me out of business; and 4) Rescuing my company from a deep financial ditch. Then there was that fifth personal thing, which at the time loomed large and was rather traumatic.

You probably guessed it by now. If you happened upon this book – even bought it – you are not really my target audience, though I am very grateful you have reached the twelfth paragraph of the introduction. I encourage you to read on. I would offer a money-back guarantee, but that would be a charlatan's promise.

Most failed writers eventually talk of only writing for themselves.

Hogwash. They write for the masses, and are sorely disappointed when the only readers are their mothers; and maybe the uncle who is laid up in the hospital with a hernia and has nothing else to read. However, and I kid you not, this work is written for those five children and five grandchildren and children and grandchildren yet to be born.

It is also written for my wife, Olga, whom I met late in life after two marriages, neither of which I would describe as failed unions but merely, in the end, one ran out of gas (my fault) and the other was nuked while I figuratively slept. My first ex I often describe as a saint, because she was by far the better partner in our marriage. It lasted nearly 30 years. The other marriage I obviously failed in other ways, but for the life of me I don't know how. It did, however, give me two of five greatest all time children.

Olga rescued me when I was in despair. That made us more than lovers but also great friends and confidants. One should not be so happy at this stage in life. Perhaps that is why I am, indeed, the optimistic alien and it is to her I dedicate this book.

J. Michael Willard
May 9, 2010 (My 65th Birthday)

Chapter

I

Why Are We Here?

I came to Kyiv, Ukraine from America in 1994 expecting to stay a year. I never left. What is it about a place that seems so strange in the beginning but that grows on you and sticks to you like gray and silver Spanish moss, and which does, indeed, become part of your planetary being?

The very real but myth-gilded Casablanca was everyman's expat town, and the sad-eyed fellow who sat at the table at Rick's Place was the expat in all of us, leaving a question that forever hangs like a cartoon balloon over our heads: Why are we here? Why have we chosen Kyiv, so far from our native countries, our native cities, our families, our friends?

For me, as this book relates, I was in flight from a rather boring PR job in Washington D.C. Having run my own company the decade before, living on my boat on the Potomac River could not generate sufficient excitement to anchor me to an international public relations firm and the exaggerated quest for, as it is known, the billable hour. It was not that it was fake or phony, it was merely corporate life, and I harkened back to the "Man in the Gray Flannel Suit" and wondered if I had become he, without the still vulnerable but granite like visage of the starring actor, Gregory Peck.

But was there more? Of course there was. Every expat has a story, and as the song goes, he or she is a "walking contradiction, partly truth and partly fiction…"

Having owned houses, a cabin cruiser, a plane, an assortment of colorful sports cars and even the proverbial pony, I found myself in 1994 without house, boat, sports car, plane or even equine companionship. Early in Ukraine, all I owned was my $101 a day expense allowance from the government. The salary was sent stateside to meet a lifetime of responsibilities.

There was also the looming divorce I didn't know but suspected would happen. There was the downturn in the business I had sold to my employees in West Virginia, and their inability to pay me for it less than a year after the deal.

Misfortune often stalks the would-be expat, you say.

There was a yearning for excitement, and the genuine feeling the USAID-sponsored market reform education program I led in Ukraine actually was doing some good, and not a waste of taxpayer money. The verdict is still probably out on that one.

All this made sense at the time, though, to a fellow bumping up against the bubble age of 50, that time when you either have made or will make something of your life, or you sink into satisfied but under-funded retirement, a simple goal to which some aspire.

But what now, more than 15 years on? What has weighted me down like the pull of a big anvil around my neck, existing as I do on the third floor of an apartment building in the shadow of St. Sophia church? What do I think on a clear as blue ice weekend day as I puff a Cohiba from my balcony and watch time being committed?

What is the lure of this city, Kyiv? This country, Ukraine?

In Casablanca, the police captain poses the question with a twinkle in his eye, "Rick, I would like to think you killed a man. It's the romantic in me." Rick replies he came for his health, "the waters"; and when told they were in the desert, he deadpanned, "I was misinformed." I must also have come for "the waters."

In the backyard of your mind, you always wonder if the expat sitting across from you asking about the possibilities of employment has his mug on a post office wall back home with the notation "wanted" at the bottom and even a possible mention of reward.

A few years back, an expat employee – no longer in Ukraine – came to me and confessed a conceivable sin that was neither illegal nor, for that matter, immoral, but he wanted to get it off his chest. He thought I might find out from a third party and actually give a damn.

"You've told me more than I want to hear," I said. "We're sort of like the French Foreign Legion. The past is the past." We are all running to or from something or someone.

Over the years and on several occasions both from other expatriates and Ukrainians, I have heard a nebulous line of thinking that we are here because we couldn't make it anywhere else. In other words, by definition, an expat in Ukraine is a failure in life.

Perhaps it is my ego, but I believe this is a silly notion. If it is not, we are a sad ship of fools, indeed.

I am reminded of Jed Sunden, who started a newspaper from scratch and now has a publishing empire. In 2009 he sold a recession-slim weekly newspaper, the Kyiv Post, for more than a million dollars to another expat, Mohammad Zahoor, a Pakistani who held a British passport. Zahoor came to Ukraine as a student, got into the steel business, and ended up a billionaire. And of Mike Perry, who launched a successful construction company in a hostile climate, or the Scottish clan at Pulse, who keep on ticking and building like the Energizer bunny. Or Guillermo Schmitt, brought to Ukraine at age 63 to do what he had done for newspapers in Argentina: revive them. For a while, of course, there was Eric, the East German so famous he needed only one name. His restaurants grew like mushrooms in a summer rain, until they didn't anymore, and then, some say, he went on the lam from creditors. Word on the street is that he's back now.

One might say that Willard guy hasn't faired that badly, what with a business that has expanded to several countries despite some goofy ideas from the fellow whose name is on the door. But all is subjective – and fleeting.

I like to think the entrepreneur is the true expat. Other foreigners are merely getting off the bus for a 20-minute sandwich break, only to rejoin the tour when the engine cranks up. Entrepreneurs have an emotional and monetary commitment, not easily extractable.

The true expat is galled when he hears other so-called expats talk about "these people" in a derogatory way. The true expat guy, with his 20-years or younger girlfriend or wife, looks on the tourist "sexpat" with wry contempt. Worse than that: We don't like the bastards.

When I came to Ukraine, I intended to stay a year. I am now a veteran of 16 years in the region. I have lived in Kyiv longer than I have ever lived in any place in my life. Still, I am asked, "When will you be going home?"

"Home?" I reply.

Or, as Rick Blaine said with an air of acceptance when told he should help the freedom fighter Victor Laszlo or the man would die in Casablanca: "What of it. I'm going to die in Casablanca. It's a good spot for it."

The same is true for Ukraine.

Chapter
2

Goodbye to Mountain Mamma

Of all the places on my 38-foot Chris Craft Corinthian, I liked the forward V-berth the best. It was here I could lie awake at night, feel gently lapping waves, and dream about being somewhere else. That somewhere could be anywhere, everywhere. I was approaching 50 at 80 miles an hour, and was miserably satisfied, an odd combination of words that exactly described my near-comatose condition.

It wasn't that I didn't like life on a boat, particularly at the Gangplank Marina on the Washington Channel of the Potomac River. On weekends I slept in late, read the Washington Post and a dozen magazines, and caught a movie in the afternoon. I lived for the velvety curtain of a theater, and a biggest box of popcorn sold. Some people do pills. I do popcorn. If the world as we know it is about to end, and everyone is in huge shelters underground, I want there to be plenty of popcorn, the kind you can get at the Rialto.

Living on a boat in a marina is sort of like living in a trailer park in what was called back in the 50s and 60s a trailer court. From the time I was seven until I was 12, my family lived in a 39-foot Platt trailer that my father pulled across country with a 1950 Studebaker. I loved the nomadic life, even though I rarely moved my boat from its slip on "G" dock. However, it was a life at dead calm.

If you have ever been 49, it's not like 39 or 29. It is the time when you start thinking you are your father, though not as genuine or as smart. Mine died at age 53, but it wasn't the cliché of a stalking mortality that bothered me. It was a sense that I had accomplished so little in a half century on the planet. Sand was moving through the hourglass at incredible speed.

Except for an occasional lapse of morality, I had not hurt anyone, and to the person I had hurt the most, I was sufficiently remorseful, or as remorseful as I felt I could be. But I had taken up space, vertical real estate. While I was not a lush, I was in training to be. Jack Daniels was a pal, and though I would count the fat grams on packages at the Safeway in D.C.'s Southwest, I would also go on an inspired binge and gulp down a half-gallon of Fudge Ripple ice cream. My belly button was a mysterious object to me. I had not seen it for a few years without the aid of a mirror. But I loved that boat, and the smoke of a good cigar. Toss in an affordable whiskey or sour mash and I was content, or at least reasonably so. That's why I probably came up with miserably satisfied.

There were some accomplishments over those nearly 50 years. I was told I was – up to a certain year – the youngest state bureau manager ever for the now skeletal wire service, United Press International. I had been first a press secretary and then the director of the U.S. Senate Democratic Leader's office at 31. I had helped a Rockefeller, John D. No. 4, make it to the United States Senate, and I had led an award-winning (aren't they all?) public relations and advertising company in West Virginia. By some accounts, I was a minor league phenomenon who had done fairly well in the backwaters of life. I had been at an important senator's side when he met with kings and queens and prime ministers. My friend Russell Isaacs of Charleston, West Virginia, who was about 60 at the time, complained to me one evening that he was in the twilight of a mediocre career. Maybe that was the stage I was at approaching 50. That's when people really start telling war stories.

I don't believe storytelling has much currency. I'm not writing about Uncle Remus stories, or O. Henry or Edgar Allen Poe. I'm speaking about people who live their lives talking about what happened 20 or 30 years ago. That's a fool's trap. It makes you look and feel musty. Maybe that's why I watch VH1 and seek adventures on most days. I don't want to grow stale. I don't want anyone to ever say "he used to be somebody a long time ago." I would rather them say I never was anyone.

I once heard the line about "being someone once" after a speech Pierre Salinger, the former press secretary to President Kennedy and former ABC Paris newsman, gave at a downtown Washington hotel. The speech was sparsely attended, and these two late 20-something banana brains were critiquing it as if they had actually accomplished something in their lives. I thought Pierre was mostly a blowhard, but he had at least been in the right place at the right time. He was an accidental celebrity, which is more than most of us are. And he was still plugging away in his mid-70s when I worked with him during his brief stint at the public relations agency Burson-Marsteller.

By the time I got to Washington the second time, most of my exploits had taken place years earlier. Most recently, I had sold my West Virginia advertising and public relations business to my employees. It was September 1993, and I was tired of struggling in a state that should have been named after a destructive hurricane – maybe Katrina, that was a bad one. America has its economic cycles, but West Virginia has simply a recession cycle, and no amount of coaxing and adjusting by the Federal Reserve has the same impact on my adopted home state as it does the rest of the country. I was also tired of swimming in a business the size of a plastic swimming pool, the kind used by toddlers. My appetite was for the entire spa (My daughter, now 40, tells me how she wants to become famous. "Get in line," I say.).

I landed in West Virginia by virtue of one of those life-defining moments. Having worked for Senate Democratic Leader Robert Byrd for nearly eight years, I could finish his sentences. I knew his speeches by heart because I had written many of them. In fact, I felt I had become him. His bad qualities latched on to me like barnacles on the bottom of a boat, and his best qualities – and he had many – eluded me like spirits that hover but never land.

Besides, I was sure that this major domo relationship with the Leader – and that is what we called him – had made me susceptible to panic attacks, and that which had been episodic gradually was happening on a daily basis. My first panic attack occurred in 1982 when I was running five miles on the C&O towpath that borders the Potomac River near Shepherdstown, West Virginia. I felt sure I was having a heart attack, and wondered why I was not stone cold dead since I was a good two miles from my car and had to walk back, hyperventilating all the way. When I got home, my wife drove her shaking husband to the Martinsburg Hospital emergency room, where they gave me an electrocardiogram. The doctor explained I had had a panic attack and prescribed Tranxene. About five years later, I graduated to Xanax.

One night, taking the train from the District of Columbia to Brunswick, Maryland, about 18 miles from my home in Shepherdstown, I had a panic attack and had to force myself to get off at my stop. For a full five minutes I was frozen in my seat. I was lucky that Brunswick was the end of the line for this particular milk run; otherwise I might have stayed on until Chicago, if the train went that far. Today I don't have panic attacks. I don't think they are gone, merely disappeared behind a convenient tree. However, I gave up Tranxene and Xanax long ago for Coca-Cola Light and Georgian, as in the country, Borjomi water.

In 1983, an opportunity came my way. Patrick Griffin, a friend and former Secretary of the U.S. Senate who had recently left Capitol Hill, asked me if I would be communications director for Gov.

John D. Rockefeller IV's campaign for the Senate. Pat had started a lobbying/public affairs company, and was helping the Rockefeller people raise money for the campaign. It took me less than a day to say "yes", and then to actually push for the job. It would be a transitional year, slowly easing my way from politics to civilian life.

I have always made rather quick career decisions, and have been lucky that most appear to have been the right decisions. I just never liked talking something to death. Most all job decisions were based on an ambitious streak, though I never burned any bridges behind me. In fact, I generally took the time to repair the bridge and put a nice coat of paint on it before crossing. My exit letters could have been put to song. Sen. Robert Byrd, for a very long time, had my resignation letter posted on the wall outside his office. I never knew this until I visited him in 2004, and he pointed it out to me. Sadly, the good senator, my friend and my mentor, died in June 2010.

Early in my career, with a wife and a new child to support, I quit my job at the *Tampa Times* in the hope *United Press International* would hire me. There were no guarantees, for UPI had just hired away a reporter from the staff, and the only way I had a chance was to actually quit. I think I was unemployed for about 24 hours. When I shifted careers and took a job with Sen. Byrd, it was a decision made prior to being interviewed for the job. I just felt it was an experience I could not pass up.

This is not a book about my life in West Virginia. I chronicled much of it in an earlier work titled *The Flak*, which was a combination autobiographical/lessons in public relations book. However, I have related the previous merely to bring you up to date. In all, I have managed to pack six careers into about 45 work years. It has seemed that restlessness usually sets in the eighth or tenth year of each, and I move on. These passages can best be segmented as follows: journalist, age 22-31; political aide, 31-39; West Virginia entrepreneur, 39-48; public relations executive, 48-53; Eastern

European entrepreneur, 53 until present. I guess I should be packing my bags now. However, this last gig brings something new and challenging every day, and inside of one big job is multiple careers in advertising, public relations, management, human resources, promotions – you name it. Alas, I think I will stay put so long as not swept away by revolution or age. But maybe not.

(In October 2010 I sold 75 per cent of my company to All About Brands of London, a company run by a colleague and friend, Allan Biggar. Allan was someone I had observed over the years as a talented manager when he had held numerous leadership positions with the worldwide PR firm, Burson-Marsteller. Our share agreement granted total independence to Willard, and our offices in Kiev, Moscow and Istanbul. I was named a "roving ambassador" for All About Brands and given mentoring responsibilities throughout the AAB system, which included London, Abu Dhabi and Mumbai at that time. I remained chairman of Willard.)

As for my company in West Virginia, it took nearly two years for my former employees to put it in a ditch, but bankrupt it they did. They were good passengers, but given the responsibility of steering, they were as wobbly as a bicycle with bent spokes. At its height, the business barely broke a million and change, but it had made a good life for my family and me for the better part of a decade. The business I had labored over, in the final accounting, delivered unto me a couple thousands dollars, a pittance after so long. I didn't regret it though. There wasn't really anything to regret. There were good people at that company, and I liked them all. Running a business, however, was beyond them.

Which brings me to swaying back and forth in the V-berth of my boat, The *Kelly Dawn* (named for my eldest daughter), listening to the gurgle of the various pumps and having this miserably satisfied life and talking in oxymorons.

The truth is, though I have written three books that relate

to public relations, I was not cut from that cloth. PR people are gregarious. They don't just talk about the weather; they explain the weather in glorious detail, all the while at social functions balancing a wine glass and a plate of dainty finger food. I can't do that. I rarely drink wine. Many PR people seem to have this kinetic energy about that which is as deep as table dust. Public relations – advertising for that matter – is something to which I just gravitated, sort of like a penny magnet. I don't even attempt to compare either profession to that of a caregiver, a country doctor, a legal aid lawyer, or, for that matter, an auto mechanic. I wouldn't know which automobile body cavity in which to insert an oil stick. When it comes to pitching a story to a journalist – unless it is really a bell-ringer – I am the world's worst. I assume this comes from being a reporter and really knowing what makes news and what doesn't. I can't sell a phony story without breaking out in laughter.

However, I do believe both advertising and PR are noble professions, so long as you are not so superficial in the job that you shine like worn cotton.

The fact is, PR doesn't equate with brain surgery, though it educates people on the topic. It is not rocket science, but the publication of such can encourage our youth to go into the field. In other words, it is what you make of it, and I like to think I have done my best in this regard. True, I have been on both sides of the tobacco issue. I fought long and hard with Blue Cross/Blue Shield against kids under 16 being allowed to buy snuff or smokeless tobacco. However, I also fought to keep regressive taxes off cigarettes and have worked with Philip Morris in Ukraine to encourage current smokers to switch to Bond Street. I can justify this in my mind as being libertarian and honest – though some might conside not noble.

It should be noted that I don't consider myself a PR man over an ad man, though I realize that combining the two drives the purist up a wall. The fact of life is the entire communications field is melding into one. When it comes down to it, it is really all about the effective delivery of messages to target audiences. New technologies to accomplish this are coming to the forefront every day.

In the brave new world of 1984, we first opened the doors of Willard & Arnold Communications as a Charleston, West Virginia-based public relations firm. The first client to walk through the door was the local manager of Holiday Inns. He didn't need a PR proposal. He was in desperate need of a radio spot on his new Mesquite Grill. So, we hung out another shingle. I penned the script and sent it to a friend to add the sizzle and other sound effects. It won us our first award, but the bar at that particular competition was fairly low.

I was not originally from West Virginia. I adopted the state because I was connected politically to it through Sen. Robert Byrd, and I worked there for UPI before I went to Washington. Later, I returned and set up my own shop. My father was an Air Force Sergeant and home could be anyplace. We all just sort of ended up during the wonder years in Orlando, Florida, home of Mickey Mouse. My 88-year-old mother still lives there.

I came from a news background, having sat at the city desk of the *Orlando Sentinel* at age 19 while still in college. By the time I was 22 and out of the University of Florida, I had worked for several dailies on weekends and in the summers. I remember my first byline, a short article on country music legend Johnny Cash not showing up for a performance in Orlando, something that happened from time to time with Mr. Cash. The next day, I trotted off to class proud of my effort and wondering how many fellow students at the university saw my name in print. The answer, apparently, was zero. I learned that you do not become famous in a 12-point Times Roman font. Later, I interviewed Cash back stage of the Grand Ole Opry when I wrote a national music column for UPI.

I talked, walked and looked like a veteran by the time I took a first full-time job with the *Tampa Times*, covering the Federal beat, which consisted of a juxtaposition of one day reporting on Social Security and on another day gangsters that were the target of State's Attorney E.J. Salcines. For three weeks, I even found myself in Adana, Turkey, covering NATO exercises. All the while, my objective was not to write THE great American novel, but merely to pen one sufficiently interesting and publishable to put something other than canned tuna on the dinner table. I was making $105 a week, and my wife, Becky, spent a grand total of $8 a week for groceries. Looking back, it was a happy and exciting world in which I lived, though a limited one.

To my knowledge, I had nothing against public relations people. They dressed better than I did and had better cars. However, I didn't respect them. How could someone pick as a role-model a seersucker-suited chap with big ears who represented the National Flower Association, and who dropped off goofy press releases at city desk about it being National Floral Week.

"Who gives a shit," Sentinel editor Dan Hinson would crack, and we would muse over the next 10 minutes how we knights of the city desk would never fall into such disrepute. With public relations people you might have a casual conversation, but you would never tell anyone about it, and you certainly wouldn't invite them to the pool hall, or even for a beer. We felt we were special, we chroniclers of mayhem and conflict, whether it be covering what was generally known as the "cop shop" or, the slightly more genteel politics. We were characters per se, maybe not as Damon Runyun-esque as we would have liked to believe, but characters all the same.

As for advertising, that is actually what it says on my diploma: Bachelor of Science in Advertising. But I never intended to go that direction. I had played Russian roulette with the curriculum and was about to be tossed out of the university for poor grades. Then, I discovered in the journalism school a semi-academic sequence that actually needed students, the world of advertising. I am one of the few people I have known in the advertising game who ever actually got a degree in advertising. It is sort of like getting a degree in building paper airplanes. Still, it was a union card I punched.

After a 10-year career as a reporter (counting part-time jobs) – several of those spent as a music columnist in Nashville, Tennessee, and several more spent as a bureau chief of UPI in Kentucky and then West Virginia – I traded up, as my friend and former *U.S. News and World Report* editor Lewis Lord would say. I went into politics. Actually, when I told Lewis of my transition, I said pitifully, "I sold out." "No," he replied, "you cashed in." Technically, that wasn't entirely true, but it makes for a good story.

When I accepted the job with Sen. Byrd, I had no idea I would spend the next eight years globetrotting around the world with him, most often with him serving as emissary of then-President Carter. When he stopped traveling, I went back on the road, leading various staff delegations to Central America, which in certain spots in the early 1980s was a rather bellicose area to traverse. About this time, I figured my Senate career was bogging down, and the only thing that interested me was seeking adventure in El Salvador or Nicaragua where the Intelligence and Policy staff groups I led would meet with both national leaders and guerilla leaders, once even on the same day.

One day, when I returned from my latest trip to El Salvador and was working feverishly to put together a committee report on findings, Byrd called me into his office. He looked at me, and said with climatic sincerity, "Mike, I really don't give a damn about Central America."

It was obvious it was election time, and the election cycle blues had kicked in. Byrd always won by at least 70 per cent of the vote, and pondered openly why the other 30 per cent could have been so mistaken or, perhaps, careless. The election of 1982 was no exception. I hung around to see Byrd re-elected, again by 70 per cent, and moved on to another election, that of Gov. Rockefeller to the U.S. Senate.

I could dwell on that race for the rest of the book, but, if you have carefully read the title, it is about an alien, not in the sense of scary monsters from the netherworlds, but your common, garden-variety expatriate.

At this moment, I can almost hear the moan from the small audience of readers I have somehow corralled. "Oh, my god, not another expat book." I realize that to hook you into reading this narrative I probably have to offer up dark intrigue, plenty of sex, a Herculean power struggle and a measure of violence. I will try, with the possible exception of violence, which I am generally against.

However, as I write these words, Russia is marching across the Republic of Georgia, bringing considerable military might to bear against a country that had the audacity to proclaim itself a democracy and seek membership in the North Atlantic Treaty Organization (NATO). Thus far, more than 2,000 people have died in the breakaway territory of South Ossetia and in Georgia. At least that is the claim. In this case, the Georgians acted rather foolishly in a foray into South Ossetia, a territory where many claim Russian citizenship and hold Russian passports. In other words, the Big Bear became angry, and Georgia gave it a perfect opportunity to hold a clinic in a violent form of realpolitik (The incursion lasted only five days. Russian Prime Minister Putin had made his point).

I am rather interested in these things, and have been for the last 16 years. This is my neighborhood. I would prefer to keep it quiet in my latter years. I have business both in Russia and Ukraine (as well as Turkey), and don't want to be part of someone else's political agenda. Metaphorically, I am Rick Blaine in Casablanca, running a saloon.

Turning the clock back, I am again lying in my V-berth, thinking big thoughts and feeling miserably satisfied. It is late at night, and

I have turned in after sucking down two tumblers of Jack Daniels while on deck of the *Kelly Dawn*, where I had listened to Bob Marley and the Wailers, and watched planes fly over the Washington Monument, landing at what would become Ronald Reagan Washington National Airport.

Soon it would be 7 a.m. and I would catch a taxi downtown to the offices of Burson-Marsteller, a worldwide public relations firm where I was the media director and a senior vice president. It was a good job, a prestigious one working for one of the best PR firms on the globe. With as much gray hair as I had, I was lucky to land it in the twilight of a career. More and more, PR had become the field of the 20-somethings nudging into the 30-somethings. I hated it. In the 100-person Washington shop of B-M, I was the second-oldest person. When Harold Burson, a gentlemanly giant of PR who was in his early 70s at that time, came to visit from New York, I was the third-oldest.

From one view, it was a dream job. The people I worked with and for were terrific, and I was conducting media and crisis trainings that gave me sufficient confidence to write two books about the subjects a few years later. However, the job lacked the tightrope excitement of owning my own company. I found the regimen of filling out time sheets to the quarter hour a more creative task than the job itself. When it came right down to it, the only thing I liked about my job was leaving it in the evening for the refuge of my boat, and the camaraderie of the Gang Plank Marina. I liked the people at Burson-Marsteller. I even liked the company as an institution. It simply wasn't the job for me at this particular and peculiar time of my life. Outside my own little media group world of perhaps a dozen, it brought back all those thoughts as a newsman of what I didn't like about PR people.

Then, as the narrator in the movie *Captain Blood* gushed: "Fate Intervened."

A few months after I landed at Burson-Marsteller, courtesy of old friend Gary Auxier, who was the chief operating officer of the Washington office, the company urged its staff to take a one-time offer of an early out. In other words, retirement. It seemed the industry was bedeviled by a nationwide downturn, and public relations budgets were often the first to go. It was a handsome offer for those who had been at the company for some time, and to B-M's disappointment, some who they wanted to keep jumped ship.

I, being the new fellow on board, was safe; but I had to scramble to show my value, and I did that by raising the visibility of the media group and my own profile in the company. I ran a rather successful PR campaign for my own group, even producing a short video on a shoestring. By the end of summer, I was the only senior vice president invited to the company's worldwide conference of senior staff, mostly executive vice presidents and up, at Lansdowne in Northern Virginia. Even Gary, who had known me when we were fishing buddies back when I headed up UPI in Kentucky and he worked for the Ashland, Kentucky paper, was surprised when I leapfrogged others in a relatively short time span. I had accomplished my goal of getting noticed by the president of the Washington office, Don Cogman, and it was he who selected me for the conference.

One evening in late August, however, Gary, who had a much larger office down the hall from mine, called and suggested that the two of us go for a drink. Gary often summoned me to his office in the evening. He kept a bottle of Dewar's Scotch in a drawer. This time, though, he said let's go out to a place just around the corner, aptly called "Gary's".

This was a little unusual, and I said to myself, "This is it. I am being fired by my best friend."

They (the human resources books) always suggest taking the victim to a crowded place to give the axe on the assumption the victim will be gentleman enough not to make a scene and scream to high heaven about the unfairness of it all. It was a Friday evening, the perfect day for a firing. All the human resources department stars were lined up just so. Recession in the PR business, offer to go for a drink, place just next door, Friday evening. Yep, the blade was falling even as I was stuffing a few papers into my briefcase to meet up with Gary.

Gary's Bar was only around the corner, and we walked along in silence. It was drizzling rain, as I remember, but it could have been a gully-washer. This motion picture was running continuously through my mind. How would I tell my then-wife that she was going to have to return to $8 a week grocery shopping – and the price of tuna in nearly 30 years had risen enormously? At this point, there was no option of returning to my company in West Virginia.

In the year with B-M, I had managed to save only $2,000. My West Virginia company where I still was listed as chairman and perhaps simply missing in action, was meandering its way toward a bankruptcy filing, and finally did a year later. My Individual Retirement Account with B-M was so new the ink had not dried on the forms. In all, financially, I was a tearjerker of a country ballad being nose-sung by my old friend Little Jimmy Dickens.

At Gary's Bar, Gary ordered his traditional Dewar's, and I, numb and not thinking creatively, did the same. I could tell Gary had something to say, but it wasn't quite coming out. It was as if he needed the lubricant to get the difficult words flowing. He started to say something profound, but then would retreat back to the safety of some little incident that happened during the day or perhaps 20 years earlier.

So, I charged forth, "Gary, you have something on your mind. What is it?" I have never had any sense of delayed gratification or delayed non-gratification for that matter. I want bad news early and between the eyes, though not often.

"How would you like to go to Ukraine?" he deadpanned.

I was not sure whether I heard him right. Gary has a whisper soft voice, and my ears, after spending the better part of one year traveling around West Virginia in a helicopter with Gov. Rockefeller and without ear protection, had lost some lower pitches.

"What?"

"The Ukraine," he said, meaning the newly independent nation of Ukraine, which correctly is spoken without the "the" that so many continue to still put in front of it.

"Let's have another drink," I replied, but breathed a sigh that could be heard in Texas. I had been continuously employed at something since age 12 when I sold Flowers' Donuts door-to-door in the Englewood subdivision in Orlando. Being pastured to unemployment land at age 49 was not something that I felt would build character.

Gary went on to explain that – if I could land the job, and that was a big if – I would lead one of the largest U.S. governmental aid programs in the world from Kyiv. However, I would have to undergo several interviews at USAID, and there was no guarantee the job would be mine. After all, I had spent little time out of the country, and I didn't speak Russian, much more specifically Ukrainian. In other words, my resume was pretty thin to go off globetrotting.

After the second drink, I asked the most geographically challenged question: "Where's Ukraine?"

"I don't know," Gary replied. "It's one of those countries near Russia."

In life, as I have written in my book for gray-hairs like me, *The Portfolio Bubble, Surviving Professionally at 60*, one needs agents and advocates, particularly in what business philosopher Charles Handy calls the "third stage", a period roughly 25 years away from kick the bucket time. People like me have to know how to use these agents and advocates, and to be properly appreciative when they come through.

Gary had always come through. We had lived next door to one another in Shelbyville, Kentucky. He has always been there for me, and, I would like to believe, me for him. There are people who would need a Microsoft Excel file to calculate all their "good" friends. I need fingers, but not all 10. I believe in having a few good friends, ones that don't laugh at you the next day when you confessed to an embarrassing semi-moment while drinking the night before. The most pertinent question among guys might be: "Who would you like to sleep with at work – if you knew your wife wouldn't catch you?"

At this time, Gary was undergoing his own career crises. He had been overlooked as president of B-M Washington because a rival just happened to generate more business in this particular year. For his part, Gary had contributed mightily to the agency's coffers, having been a rain man when he was senior account leader for Philip Morris.

"Well," said Gary, "are you interested?"

A prudent person would think twice about moving to the other side of the world, a place that during the 1990s had claimed the title The Wild East. A prudent man would think first of how this was going to impact close family members and other responsibilities on the home front.

Prudence is a sissy's name.

"Yeah, sure," I replied. "What do I do next?"

The Whiskey Legend

It seems to me, if I speak true,
I did not choose this place,

A decision came in a whirlwind,
 I was sent to Ukraine post haste.

The blame if at all lies for sure,
At a dimly lit bar named Gary's
Suppose could have happened anywhere,
For just up the street was Harry's.

But Gary's was the place I recall,
For it was raining, so not to tarry,
The fact was the fellow I was with,
Was strangely also named Gary.

We had one whiskey, then another,
And he popped the question so weird,
How about going to Ukraine, he said,
Thinking it was something I feared.

Now I was bored to death it seems,
And I was looking for something more risky,
So what I did next is legend for sure,
I asked for another double whiskey.

Where's Ukraine? I finally asked,
And he admitted he was not sure,
 But I was looking for excitement,
And any exotic locale was a lure.

What's your decision, he finally asked,
And by this time I was fairly misty,
I leaned back and bellowed it oh, so loud,
Hell, yes, and I'll take another whiskey.

Chapter
3

Landing the Fish

So, I began my quest to land a job in a land of which I was not familiar and had to head to an atlas to even locate. My view of Eastern Europe was also clouded by a trip to Moscow and what was then Leningrad (now St. Petersburg) 15 years earlier in 1979 with my boss, Sen. Robert Byrd. Byrd was there to discuss a nuclear arms limitation treaty with the Soviets. I was at his side.

At that time, Moscow was totally unlike it is today. Today it is garish but has a certain electricity to it that makes it one of the most exciting capitals on earth. Then, Moscow was gray, not a bright cat's eye gray, but the color of sadness. The people seemed never to smile. But, it was too late for me to even think of second thoughts. The mere whiff of a change of scenery had sent my wanderlust into overdrive. It happens.

In the 1970s, I had twice hitchhiked and taken bus trips around America, even though I was a fully-grown man of 31, had a wife and two children, and all the responsibilities that come with it. I had set out alone each time, as I did later when I would go backpacking in the mountains. Once, I initiated a training exercise by walking to my cabin in the Shenandoah Valley, about 110 miles from my Northern Virginia townhouse. I was training for a walk around the world, and had planned it down to the last detail, giving considerations for climate, terrain and hostile areas. None of those elements deterred me. It was simply that after my 100-mile walk, my feet were bloody, and the revelation hit me that there were less painful ways to prove my manhood.

However, each time even the momentary discomfort of boredom struck, I grabbed my backpack and headed to the door, usually for just a weekend break. When a child and our military family moved from city to city, state to state, I was always ready. It was simply a new opportunity to reinvent myself at a different venue. In the first grade, I changed schools three times. I went to three different high schools. If at one I weren't sufficiently talented to land a starter's job on the football team, I would get a second chance at the next. If at one I weren't the most popular guy around, I could strive for that goal with a change of scenery. In truth, I rarely achieved it.

In other words, I was metabolically, genetically and psychologically always ready for a change. It was the chlorophyll that led to my personal synthesis, causing me to blossom into the contradictory and sometimes delusional character I became. But, for the most part, I am comfortable with that. While subject to fits of minor depression, my overriding aura is one of, perhaps, benighted optimism. The condition is rarely if ever fatal, and can lead to interesting experiences. Hence, the title for this book.

It was obvious I took a taxi back to the Gangplank Marina after my discussion with Gary, but I was so engrossed in dreamy thoughts of turning a new page that I did life's little deeds, like showering, brushing teeth, even pouring a drink, without scratching into my subconscious. That subconscious already had me in Eastern Europe.

But it was not going to be so easy. I had several high hurdles to jump, climb over or otherwise find a way around. The first was easy, and was on my home turf.

Kirby Jones was several years older than I, and had had a colorful career as an aide to the late Sen. Robert Kennedy. Among his acquaintances was Cuba's Fidel Castro. The two were on a first name basis. In a very conservative company such as Burson-Marsteller, Jones was one of several with liberal credentials. I liked him as a character and a friend. It was Kirby who had suggested to Gary that it would be helpful to B-M if we could put a project manager on a USAID education program in Ukraine. Gary, forever looking out for the people who were close to him, recommended me for the job.

Aside from Gary, Kirby was who I was closest to in my one year at Burson-Marsteller Washington. Perhaps it was because of the proximity of age, but I think it was more a kindred spirit. I loved baseball. Kirby was a baseball fanatic and even attended fantasy baseball camps. I was generally considered more liberal than most – even after running a small business in the forever recession-ridden mountains of West Virginia.

It was Kirby who convinced John F. Kennedy's press secretary, Pierre Salinger, to sign up with Burson, which, while interesting, probably did B-M no favors and didn't help Kirby. By this time, Salinger was well into high-profile conspiracy theories and exaggerated his ability to generate business. He also puffed on large cigars and caused a haze of smoke to waft through the office, which was okay with me as a discreet cigar smoker, but caused many to complain. Often, Salinger would call me up one floor to his office to chat about his latest idea on some arcane subject that had nothing to do with moving commerce along, or at least commerce as B-M saw it. I dutifully went, but both Kirby and Gary asked that I report to them before acting on any of Salinger's initiatives.

"This should be a breeze for you," Kirby said, speaking of an afternoon meeting he had arranged for me with an official of USAID. "It will be with the same person who brought the Russian privatization team through here two weeks ago. Remember, you sat in on that meeting."

"Kirby, I sat in." I replied. "But it was under protest. You needed a body. I was available. During the entire meeting I was trying to fill in my goddamn timesheet from the week before. I didn't pay any attention to the guy. I never thought I would need to."

"Don't worry, you'll ace this interview." His confidence in me was not comforting. I suddenly began to worry about questions directly related to the meeting, questions such as "tell me about Russia's privatization program."

"Well, it's happening in Russia...."

During the USAID session, I met with a fellow about my age. Though I do not recall his name, he was the exact same person in the meeting in Burson-Marsteller's office to which I paid scant attention. He was a friendly Virginian, I recall, but oozed professionalism from his pores. He obviously was a career government servant.

"I remember you," he said, right out of the box. "You were in the meeting with the Russians at Burson." I half expected him to add, "And you were the guy not paying the slightest attention."

"This is an important job, and it is a difficult job," he said, as if it were a life or death mission and we were on a movie set somewhere north of the 38th parallel. "We have to be satisfied you will perform well and represent USAID in this position. We need someone who can quickly acclimate to the job. How's your Russian?"

My Russian was as good as my French that was equal to my Swahili. In others words, the only language I spoke other than English was Pig Latin. I had taken a couple of years of Spanish in high school, and had studied some Spanish on my on, but I never considered Russian.

"I don't know Russian now, but I'm a quick study, and will start with lessons as soon as I land." I tried to out Southern his molasses accent, which was thick, thinking that if we were almost cousins, I had a better chance.

"Oh," he said, seemingly disappointed. "Okay, how much time

have you spent outside the United States which would prepare you for different cultures?"

I was inclined to say that I spent nine years in West Virginia and that surely was sufficient cultural shock to understand the most difficult of circumstances. But I didn't want to slander my home state, of which I was proud and so replied honestly, leaning into him. It was a body gesture I read about that was supposed to send a signal that I was confident, even a little cocky. My sales instincts kicked in as I envisioned myself sitting across from a prospective client.

"Other than a year in England where I went to high school, a couple of vacation trips to Europe and nearly a month in Turkey covering NATO exercises for a newspaper, I have absolutely no experience outside the U.S. with the exception of my travels with Sen. Byrd. "

"Oh," he remarked again. It was a judgmental "oh", as in why did Kirby send this aging, provincial, language-challenged boob to me. But, it could have just as easily been an approving "oh". Some people were overly impressed by the Byrd credential, especially when I started name and place dropping. It helps to toss out Vice Premier Deng or General Omar Torrijos or the Shah of Iran, even though the references were so old they had accumulated spiders' nests.

"Well, you probably learned a lot from that session we had a few weeks ago. (Uh oh, now here it comes, I thought) It was a pretty thorough briefing on the Russian privatization project, and the Ukrainian one is much the same."

I nodded my head, as If I were all knowing.

Was he assuming I learned a lot, or did he know I spent the entire time meeting B-M's bureaucratic timesheet requirements? Was he testing me, wanting me to fall into his little, silly trap? I wasn't going to giv, him the satisfaction. Perhaps I could lie and say that was my twin brother who also works at Burson-Marsteller that was at his stupid meeting.

Suddenly, he said, "That's all. We'll make a decision and get back to Kirby." He closed his notebook, gave me an obligatory handshake, and walked out.

There are some things you know, and some things you think. There are even some things you think you know. I was absolutely certain that the interview with USAID was up there with my other worst interview, the time I was adopting my two-year-old bi-racial son and the judge asked me such difficult questions as his birthday, and I stumbled. My then 8-year-old daughter came to the rescue at that time, reminding me before my wife did that his birthday was on the same day as her parent's wedding anniversary. I figured by the time I drove over Key Bridge and returned to the Burson office, Kirby would be waiting in the frame of his office door to say, "Sorry Willard, you muffed it."

Kirby was waiting, but had an unconcerned look on his face.

"I assume the fellow from USAID called," I said, walking past him to my office next door. Then, I volunteered, "I don't think it went very well."

"That's not what he told me," said Kirby. "He just said you needed to meet a couple more people before they can make up their minds. These will be the people from Price Waterhouse who currently hold the contract. You would be working with Bill Mako."

It seems that with the first hurdle, the USAID fellow had been sufficiently interested in my political and journalism background that he felt I had certain qualities that would, at least, earn me a second round of interviews. I had not leaped the hurdle in a fluid, athletic motion. I had stumbled over it, but picked it up, and then climbed over. In my own mind, I was already boots on the ground.

However, I had no idea who this Mako character was. Sounded like the name of a species of shark.

I began accumulating every scrap of paper I could on Ukraine, its politics, its geography, and its people. The country of then 52 million people (now 46 million) would decide on who would be its president in two weeks. It was between two Leonids, Kravchuk, the current president from Western Ukraine, and Kuchma, a former prime minister from Eastern Ukraine. I soon learned that former President George H.W. Bush had come to Kyiv in 1991 and delivered his widely derided "Chicken Kyiv" speech in which he argued against Ukraine aggressively asserting its independence. Bush later said his remarks were misinterpreted. He had merely warned against rampant nationalism, which, it would seem, independence movements are all about. Perhaps he got Chicken Kyiv confused with Chicken Cordon Bleu. In any event, the Independence referendum passed with 90 per cent of the vote in 1991.

By the next morning, I was nearly swimming in the Black Sea, off the coast of Crimea – at least mentally. I had found Kyiv on a map, and had traced its borders with Russia, Hungary, Poland, Belarus, Moldova, Slovakia and Romania. By now, I was probably in the 99th percentile in my knowledge of Ukraine (After nearly a year in Ukraine, I was visiting Sen. Rockefeller's office in D.C. when I ran into a friend, a former governor of West Virginia, Gaston Caperton. I waved to him from a distance. He shouted back at me," Mike you're in Russia." "No, governor," I replied, "I'm in Ukraine." He bounced back, "Yeah, I know, Russia.") .

By this time, I had all but shelved my work at Burson in an all out assault to win the job. I never cared much for time sheets, and now I just ignored them. I would either get the job in Ukraine, or sink below the poverty line. Throughout the second day of the campaign, I met with a half dozen people from Price Waterhouse who would hold my fate in their hands. While B-M would handle the market reform education program, we would be under the control of Price Waterhouse at least for the first six months. We hoped to eventually win the role outright (we did), because PW rightly insisted to USAID that it wasn't in the business of running communications programs.

One person I met with was this fellow Mako, who led the Price Waterhouse team in Ukraine and Romania. Though probably 10 to 15 years younger than I, I admired him as a consummate professional, and we at once hit it off as two colleagues who could work well together. I believe this went a long way toward me securing the job, as well as Kirby's insistence that I was the right person to move the program forward. A tall, thin man, Mako gave guidance without being overbearing. He discussed rather than told. In that regard, I would think his management style was not unlike my own. He said "please" and "thank you", which I respected. Last I heard, Mako was with the World Bank in Beijing.

Another person was also in the mix. Her name was Kyra Cheremeteff, who traced her family back to Field Marshall Boris Sheremetov, a contemporary of Peter the Great. Until the 1917 revolution, her family held holdings throughout Russia and Ukraine. A gracious and beautiful person, she had what some would call a classy and regal sounding European accent. For all her stately background, Kyra said her father had been an employee of Singer Sewing machines, an early business in Russia. Kyra worked with Kirby and was charged with helping him run Burson's emerging markets practice. On occasion she would visit the team in Ukraine.

I mention these people not simply to place names in a book. Such an account would be tedious for the reader and I doubt it would help carry the narrative. However, in a life heading toward the middle of the sixth decade, it is important to me to recognize those that gave me a boost when it was not necessarily in their immediate interest to do so. On the other hand, my hope is that I am always ready to return the favor. The problem, of course, is that most people mentioned have reached a position in life where they pull others over the finish line, and rarely need help themselves. But, I am always an email, a text message or a carrier pigeon away.

While having that toe in the Black Sea, I was, at this point, far from being approved. The fact that I had never previously shown any interest in the region, and that I didn't know "do svidaniya" from "arrivederci" harmed my case. I felt sure the USAID official with the slow as syrup-pouring drawl was just being polite with Kirby and Kyra; and that my application, indeed, was an object lesson tacked to a wall on who should not be sent on USAID assignments. After all, they probably thought, this Willard fellow probably knows a little, but this is a game for youngsters and this guy is a little too calcified when flexibility is needed for this demanding job.

And the job would be demanding. It would require a diplomatic skill I had gathered working my years in politics and traveling with Sen. Byrd around the world to sit in on meetings with world leaders. It would require an attention to detail that I frankly had overlooked much of my life. It would require the ability to lead a far-flung contingent numbering close to 200 throughout Ukraine. It would require the ability to be firm and to be *Father Knows Best* to a handful of young but brilliant expatriates who were recruited into the program.

While Becky and I were living apart, she in our Florida beach condo and me on the *Kelly Dawn*, we had not even talked about an official separation, though we had been separated semi-officially for about a month several years earlier. She had moved to Florida partly because I had chosen to be indiscreet and have an affair in Charleston, a community where clothesline conversation travels like CNN and everyone from the governor to the local sheriff to the business community knew the story, or thought they did. She deserved better, and when I asked if she wanted to move to our Flagler Beach condo she was almost giddy. By this time, she hated Charleston, and has never returned.

I would also have to leave my boat and a style of life that had given birth to a new hobby, oil painting. One day I visited the National Art Gallery and happened into a room of paintings by Egon Schiele, the Austrian expressionist whose weirdly wonderful drawings and paintings had a profound impact on me. The next day I drove over to Virginia to a hobby store and picked out a set of pastels and paper. I also bought a sketchbook and was rarely without it. A little later I graduated to oils. That was more than 400 canvasses ago.

Additionally, I had a daughter, Kelly, still in West Virginia, and a son, Rob, in the Washington, D.C. area. It wasn't simply a matter of picking up and leaving.

There was more than that. There were memories and doubts that could not be bundled up and given to some charity, like Goodwill. There were still hopes and dreams, and until Gary asked me to go with him for a drink just a few days earlier, they all were planted firmly in terra firma USA.

It was never, "My country, right or wrong", but it was my country, and, of course, these many years on, it still is. When jets commandeered by terrorists slammed into the World Trade Center towers on that September day which has since become known by numbers, I was holding an issues training session with the secretary general of the ruling Socialist Party in Bucharest, Romania. I halted the training and went back to my hotel room, watched CNN and cried.

There are episodes that can never be washed out of my hair, or showered away to float like bubbles down a drain. They are painted on my skin, invisible tattoos that perhaps only I can see. There was the quarter-century marriage; there was the relatively brief liaison, and then the pileup at the intersection of life. There were the feelings of dark remorse, which visited me like Banquo's ghost. The gauzy images that melted through the closed doors of my mind were far from pleasant thoughts. They were simply my most recent past come a-calling.

To some extent, the glimmer of Ukraine represented escape, a new adventure to shout, "I told you so" to people who had really never posed the challenge. It was my imagination that soared, mood-swing high, into pink, fluffy clouds. Here I was, approaching age 50, and still attempting to prove that I was in some way special from the several billion people who roamed the planet, most of whom seemed to have no such addiction.

But certain questions remain now, some years into the experiment that would become a way of life. Would I have pursued the position with such blue flame intensity if I knew then what I know now?

We host in our subconscious those momentary episodes that define character and the essence of life. Would I have taken the leap if I had known there would be a second and soap opera traumatic failed marriage; that there would be a monumental (at least to me) struggle for survival against WPP, one of the world's largest advertising holding companies; or, that I would be caught up in one of the so-called color revolutions in the region? These events make the highlight reel, but there were many others, including the desperate battle for relevance in a business that centers on the cult of youth.

I had not the second sight to see into the future, and so didn't know what boulders and borders lay in the path ahead of me.

Two days later, Kirby stepped into my office. "Well, pack your bags."

"USAID approved me?" I was incredulous.

"Conditionally. They want you to spend a week in Moscow first observing the program there. Seems you should have paid more attention when that Russian group came here a few weeks ago. Congratulations."

At that moment, all my anxieties and second thoughts disappeared as a page was turned in the private history of a guy named Willard. Few people get second and third chances, and I was on at least my tenth.

Funny, I thought: 43 years earlier I, along with 30 or so classmates were huddled underneath our desks at Whitehaven Elementary School in Memphis, practicing for the possible eventuality of Soviet nuclear bombs raining down on our heads.

Flashy salesman had gone from hawking aluminum siding to selling bomb shelters. A kind of paranoia gripped the land. And now, I would be preaching market reform to those same Godless commies.

What a wonderful world we live in.

Chapter
4

Moscow Purgatory

Kyiv could have been Mars. Some people thought it was.

My colleague Richard Moore, who worked at Burson at the time, bought me a short-wave radio. "You're a news junkie. You'll need this," he said, as if I were taking a walkabout to the North Pole.

My wife had read that it was important to bring syringes to Kyiv. The rumor was that the medical system was so bad, doctors had to use the same needle several times. She packed enough that if my bags had been examined I would have been thought a heroin addict.

One relative, trying to be helpful, called to ask me did I know "how cold it was over there." He had read a report that it was 14 degrees that very day, which would be rather chilly for September, except he confused the zero freezing Celsius scale with 32 degree freezing Fahrenheit.

The week before leaving for Moscow, Becky and I took a cruise to the Bahamas. Other than a quick jaunt on the riverboat Delta Queen in the early 1970s, it was the only time we had taken such an excursion. It was, in essence, a farewell cruise. It was to be the last time we would live together except for a brief month she spent in Kyiv in the dead of that first grim winter. I am told it was one of the worst winters in memory. It must have been. She never returned. I didn't blame her then, or now. My own actions had set in play an emotional perpetual motion machine that neither of us had the power, or perhaps even the will, to stop.

The day to leave came quickly, and I flew from Washington's Dulles airport via Frankfurt to Moscow, landing in a pouring rain. Moscow can be a beautiful city, but in a downpour it takes on the overwhelmingly gloomy continence of Tim Burton's Gotham metropolis. I was among several wide-eyed and bewildered foreign travelers who rode the bus that ferried us from the Delta aircraft to Sheremetov Terminal 2.

In an earlier age, I was fearless when it came to travel, hitching as I did around America, daring to venture beyond the next bend in the road, and then the next, ever curious. But at a more sedate and cautious 49, I wondered if I would be able to pick out the driver among a sea of faces waiting outside customs? Would there be a sign with my name in bold lettering, or would there have been a miscommunication, and no car, no driver, no instructions. How would I tell a taxi where I wanted to go? Had I foolishly made the blunder of my life? I chided myself for being such a pansy.

Then I saw the sign, and it was bold, and the friendly face of Sasha Shipolov, a driver for Russia's Market Reform Education program. He grabbed the largest of my luggage and we maneuvered through the crowd to his small Russian-made Lada.

The trip to Moscow had been in stark contrast to my first visit, when we landed in a Boeing 707 jet from the President's fleet, a craft that had previously been used by Secretary of State Henry Kissinger in his Middle East shuttle diplomacy a few years earlier. Several limousines pulled on to the ramp to meet us. Though it was late, a line of dignitaries, including the U.S. Ambassador, greeted us. Instead of several hundred deplaning, we numbered 12, including Sen. Byrd and his wife, Erma. We cleared customs while still on the tarmac, and were whisked to a very Soviet hotel, aptly named Sovietskaya.

It was getting dark when Sasha dropped me off at the Radisson SAS Slavyanskaya hotel just across the park from the Kyiv railway station. After checking in, with jet lag over coming me, I attempted to sleep. However, a jackhammer, a drill, and an assortment of hammers created a noisy orchestra several rooms away, and I tossed and turned. Eventually, I complained to the front desk, and was told the building was being remodeled and the racket would continue for another two hours. I surrendered and went downstairs to the lobby bar, grabbing a seat next to Americans and Brits who were in the construction business. They were discussing what I was to learn expats tend to talk about in East European bars, the three C's: costs (out of sight), chicks, and corruption. It was rather boring banter for this aging wanderer, and I was already hung-over with jet lag. I returned to my room after a single drink, and put a pillow over my head.

It wasn't until later that I learned the hotel was owned partly or mostly by Paul Tatum, Oklahoma businessman who came east to make his fortune. Tatum was somewhat of a cowboy, and somehow got on the wrong side of the wrong kind of people, including enemies at City Hall. The mid-90s was a rather violent period for Moscow, and arguments quite often were settled with automatic weapons. Tatum was gunned down in a Metro station. His killers were never found. When I lived in Kyiv, and later in Moscow for two years before returning to Kyiv, it seemed hotel owners and managers were favorite targets for assassination. I never could understand why, but three hotels in which I stayed had their owners or managers bumped off, the Grand in L'viv, and the World Trade Center and Radisson in Moscow.

It was a surreal evening, huddled as I was in a hotel room so far away from the comfort of my V-berth on the *Kelly Dawn*. Looking out over Moscow from my room, I could see the spirals of the Stalin-era buildings in the distance. Traffic moved slowly along streets bordering both sides of the Moscow River. The city was gloomy and rather depressing, enveloped by a steady drizzle. I felt as if I were in a cocoon of darkness and not at all ready for the adventures beyond my hotel door. It was Friday evening. I had the whole weekend before reporting to work as a trainee of sorts with the Moscow market reform program.

It was too late, however, to turn back. I remember setting out backpacking alone one day on Massanuten Mountain in the Shenandoah Valley. Having traversed the Appalachian Trail in the Smokey Mountain National Park with my two brothers years before, I had vowed to always backpack unaccompanied. I simply liked the solitary walk, and the challenge of spending the night in the forest alone.

I remember it being early spring and trees, fractured by an ice storm, were still down on the well-marked ridge trail. In some cases, they were simply too big to climb over, so I had to go around. It was then I heard the distinctive warning of rattlesnakes on the pathway. I froze, but it was just as dangerous to retrace my steps as it was to go forward. I put my walking stick in front of me, and put one foot in front of the other, carefully, as if a blind man trying to feel his way with a cane. That was the way it was that night at the Radisson in Moscow, I just put my cane in front of me, and stepped forward.

I awoke the next morning to a blazing sun. My attitude seemed as bright as the day, my fears having been shoved under the bed the night before. I bounded out of the hotel for an exploratory walk, coming first to the train station next door. It was here I first felt the texture of Moscow, the sights and the sounds and the smells. The smell was of country butter and sausage, and, for some reason, motor oil. Over the years, I was to become very familiar with the smell.

I traversed the nearby park, and was immediately accosted by dozens of gypsy children begging for money. I gave the first an American dollar, and that was a big mistake. They swarmed on me like bees around a honey cone. It took a while for me to extract myself from the predicament. I did so by simply looking straight ahead and walking as fast as I could. It was my first lesson with gypsies, and their tactics of distract and conquer.

After crossing the bridge over the Moscow River, I came to an eight-lane thoroughfare. I looked both ways and started to cross. Suddenly, cars were coming at me, and I scampered (lumbered is more accurate) to the narrow median strip. It seemed that out of nowhere cars were coming in either direction, colorful bullets whizzing by me, horns blaring angrily. I felt a dreaded panic attack coming on as I stood smack in the middle of this race course, pulling in my butt as best I could and sucking in my stomach. It was a full 10 minutes before I made it to the other side. Then, I saw what I should have seen, an underground passageway beneath the highway, where the sane and sensible crossed.

The experience humbled me, and I walked back to the hotel, thinking I might never venture out again without an escort. Then, there was this call from Perry Yeatman, the deputy director of the Moscow USAID education program. "Want to go to a hockey game?" she asked.

Perry was about 15 years younger than I, but was an old Russia hand. She seemed to bark orders whenever she spoke, but then everything she said seemed to make some sense. I believe it was just extreme confidence – well deserved. While Englishman Chris Fisher was the nominal head of the program, my view was that Perry, an American, did most of the work. Fisher was a few years older than me. Eventually Perry was to go back to London with Burson-Marsteller, and later land a top job at Unilever before moving on in a few years later to Kraft.

The only other time I had met Perry, I really hadn't met her. That was in the meeting I attended in Burson-Marsteller's Washington office, the time I had ignored everyone to concentrate on those damn timesheets. My initial reaction was how gracious it was for her to give up her Saturday evening to entertain me.

That night was, in reality, my first real introduction to Russia, a baptism into expat culture. It was also the beginning of my Moscow Purgatory, a way station of sorts, a sentence I had to serve as my penitence for blowing off the Washington meeting.

Before the night was over I would experience only my second hockey game ever and would attend a party with primarily young expats from across the city. We drank vodka and had a lively conversation. I became aware, rather suddenly, how much gravitas mere age brought to bear on impressionable youth. It didn't hurt that I subscribed to *Rolling Stone* magazine, or had once, long ago, drank beer in a concert trailer with the Nitty Gritty Dirt Band and Ramblin' Jack Elliott. The party was in one of those grand Russian apartment complexes where the faded walls and high ceilings appeared to be taken from a set for Dr. Zhivago. It was all rather magical for this supposedly wizened chap who had been around the track more times than Richard Petty.

As an aside, I never became a typical expat, even from that Day One. In the beginning, I went to few parties, and even gave a few. My circle of friends were Ukrainian or Russians, or just the expat group that was part of my team. Mostly I felt I had little in common with expats, particularly the Ukrainian Diaspora. Early on, they were talking symbolism such as language and flag colors, while their countrymen were making on average less than $100 month and didn't have enough to eat. I found that most in the Ukrainian Diaspora understood less about Ukraine than the fly-in, fly-out expat, and what they did know they wore on their sleeves. But, those were the early days. Even the Diaspora grew up over time.

The term expat is sort of like the term alien I have in the title of this book. It is easy to misunderstand. Expatriate conjures up a callous, smarmy sort who has no allegiance to his home country

– as in ex-patriot. Alien delivers the image of monsters and space invaders; and, in America, generally has a frontal appendage – as in illegal alien. I am not an ex-patriot, though some might say I sometimes take on the characteristics of a monster. I am a patriot. One can love an adopted country without alienating the affections of his or her home country. I am the guy who gets teary-eyed emotional and then mad when the United States is threatened.

The following Monday, I went to work in an office within stone-tossing distance from the Kremlin, right off Tverskaya Ulitza, Moscow's main Street. The Moscow market reform program was located in a jungle of offices with creaky wooden floors that one reached by maneuvering a maze of hallways from the adjoining building. The time I was there I needed a guide, usually my driver, to direct me to the office.

For four days I listened intently, receiving briefings from the Russian leadership of each aspect of the program. On that fourth day, I proclaimed myself properly educated, though in truth, the Russian program bore little resemblance to the Ukraine program. The Ukraine program was somewhat more sophisticated with more creative elements. Throughout the week, I had worked (or listened) until dark, and then a driver would take me back to the Radisson. My ritual every evening was a drink at the bar, dinner at a restaurant in the hotel and then back to the bar for a nightcap. All things considered, the Moscow purgatory was just that: marking time.

It wasn't until two years later, when I returned to Moscow to head up Burson-Marsteller's operations there and in Kyiv, that I really discovered what – if taken in just the right doses – is truly one of the world's great cities – along with London, Istanbul, Kyiv and maybe my hometown of Charleston, population 100,000 and shrinking. When one moves around as much as I did, most anywhere can legitimately be your home town. I as born in Vidalia, Georgia, but after being attached in one way or another to West Virginia for many years, I adopted it or it adopted me. After 16 years in Eastern Europe, I guess the same could be said about Kyiv.

My last night in Moscow I was to meet a tall Englishman by the name of David Payne in the Radisson bar. David had served as head of the advertising and design portion of the Ukrainian market reform program that, up until a few weeks earlier, was under the leadership of another Englishman, Martin Nunn. David was on vacation, passing through Moscow on his way to his wife's home in Nizhny Novgorod, the city called Gorky during Soviet times. It was to be a brief meeting with a crucial element in the program I was inheriting. David had already taken the initiative to write me a constructive memo on how he thought the program might be improved.

But Bill Mako of Price Waterhouse said the problems were real, not imagined, and Mako was the sort of understated fellow you had to believe unless your eyes told you his black and white were really your green and blue. In any event, I took over from Nunn, who had guided the program for about a year, and who was liked by the market reform staff.

David Payne, tall and sturdy as an oak, was about five years younger than I. He was creative when it came to developing overall ad strategy – probably one of the best in Eastern Europe, but not quite as good on the creative idea itself. On occasion, though, he would surprise all of us with a killer idea wrapped in a killer strategy. On this particular evening, I had no idea what David looked like as I cruised the bar looking for a tall English fellow who might be with his Russian girlfriend (and later wife). These were days when cell phones were a rarity, and neither David nor I had one. So, I went from barstool to barstool, table to table in a hopeless search for David. No luck. Eventually, I called both the search and the evening quits. I had to meet a driver early the next morning for an early flight to Kyiv.

At the time, I had no idea, that several years later I would form a partnership with David, and that this partnership would last 10 years before I had to dissolve it during a difficult downturn in not just the advertising business, but in most Ukrainian businesses. I later learned that David and his then girlfriend, Galina, were in another bar in the hotel. There had merely been a miscommunication. Over the years, there were to be many miscommunications and a few loud arguments, but overall, it was a good partnership, lasting longer than my second marriage.

Early the next morning, I left Moscow for my future.

Chapter
5

A Confederacy of the Well-Intentioned

Kyiv's Borispol Airport was not the glassy, relatively modern facility it is today. In fact, you picked up your baggage from a railing outside the terminal. As I was looking for my considerable luggage, Makram Abboud, an employee of Price Waterhouse, greeted me with a smile, a handshake and instructions.

Makram was the first person I met in Ukraine, and he promptly told me that Price Waterhouse had arranged an apartment, and that I would be staying with another employee who was working on the mass privatization project. Maybe I was just sleepy from a late night and an early flight, but it didn't go down well.

"Nope, sorry," I replied. "I haven't had a sleepover since Cub Scout days. Not starting now. I would much prefer a hotel until I can find an apartment."

"But it's been arranged," he stuttered.

"Then, let's find a way to un-arrange it," I said.

It was one of those glorious September days, with the sun shimmering off the Dnipro River as we crossed. I looked to the right of the Paton Bridge and looming like a colossus before me was the so-called Iron Maiden, or the titanium statute, pointing to the sky and looking majestic and menacing at the same time.

It was impressive, almost a little scary. Perhaps it was meant to intimidate.

Makram said it would take some time, but he would see what he could do about the living arrangements. In the meantime, he asked if I would mind staying my first night in the shared apartment, or at until there was time to find a permanent place.

I didn't want to be prickly, and Makram seemed like a nice fellow. He had what I would call a cautious smile, meaning a half smile that never fully forms, and stayed on his face all the time like it was set in concrete. He was in his mid-20s, and I must have seemed ancient to him, a cantankerous Neanderthal. At least, I felt, I had sent the first signal that I had arrived, and that I felt I had sufficient stature not to be pushed around on the first day of my new job.

In the final analysis, I ended up staying about a week in the shared apartment up a street jutting off from Kyiv's Independence Square. However, my roommate, the No. 2 man in Kyiv with Price Waterhouse, obliged me by being away in Moscow most of that time. This was good. He had the room with the TV set.

After stowing my bags at the apartment, Makram and a driver took me to Dom Kino, or Cinema House, a four-story building that housed the Ukraine Market Reform Education Program on the third floor. The building had cold slate floors, and on the first floor were a souvenir and book kiosk and a restaurant. There was an old woman pushing a mop over the floor. She had the face of time, and I don't remember seeing her not mopping that same floor the year and a half I was there.

Being somewhat out of shape, the three flights to my new office winded me. We're talking high-ceiling floors, about four and a half floors in most buildings. On the way up, following Makram, I attempted to capsule what I might tell my new employees. How could I establish myself from the outset as both leader and friend? I had been leading small groups most of my professional life, but the entire market reform program approached 200 people, and very few spoke English.

I am certain I was a curious spectacle as I emerged at the top of the steps, a specimen from America to guide a U.S.-funded program that heretofore had only Brits actually in charge, Martin Nunn as director, and David Payne, who headed up the design studio.

While I didn't know that much about David, Kirby Jones had told me he was a nice guy, good at his job, but had not been considered for the leadership position. I knew more about Nunn, who was popular with a segment of the Ukrainian team, and also had allies in USAID.

About 75 Ukrainians worked in the Kyiv office of the program, along with two other expats, both Americans: Peter Bejger, who oversaw the publications group, and Billy Kimball, a cynical, longhaired television consultant. I was later to bring to the program about a half-dozen other expats with the assistance of Kyra Cheremeteff, who recruited what I believed then and now was a truly exceptional group.

However, that was weeks away, and I had to greet an apprehensive crowd who, in the wake of Nunn's dismissal, were unsure of their futures. These were people who were, on average, making five times the salary of people who worked outside the American government industry, and, in some cases, had managed to get their boyfriends, sisters, cousins or in-laws connected with the program. It was nepotism run rampant. It was a situation that after a few weeks I didn't necessarily want to change, even if I could. It was simply a way of doing things in Eastern Europe. Over the years, I found that my Western business model rarely fit like a glove in Eastern Europe, more like a pair of baggy dungarees. In dealing with cultural nuances, I tried to innovatively adjust, generally coming up with a hybrid system that seemed to work relatively well.

With Bill Mako of Price Waterhouse standing beside me, I called everyone around, introduced myself, and gave what was to be the first of many talks to people I grew to care about, to admire and to respect. As I recall, I talked about the usual things, about goals, about dreams, about my philosophy of working. It probably wasn't a jump-up-and-applaud inspiring speech. I was met with a collective nervous smile. That's what people do when they are not sure how to react. My final comment was a joke, but, strangely, some remembered it years later, after the program was over and we had left the building.

"And another thing," I said with a flourish, wiping my brow with my hand. "I promise to have an elevator installed." Over the years, I made promises and kept most of them. That one, however, made in jest, was the one they remembered, and I am reminded of it still from time to time.

At the time, it was impossible to know that a half-dozen of the group would still be with me years later, and most in high positions in Willard, including the current president of advertising (Tania Spiridonova), executive vice president (Natasha Lotra), the director of media relations (Maxim Rylsky), the deputy finance director (Larisa Yanyuk), the webmaster (Igor Panchenko) and a senior art director (Igor Kovriga).

But then, in my vision, the gig was supposed to end within a 12-month span, and I would be back bobbing up and down on the *Kelly Dawn* on the Washington channel of the Potomac River. It was impossible to know that I would be in Kyiv long enough see the calamities that befall families, the divorces, the sickness, as well as the significant life achievements, including watching kids grow, marriages happen and sons and daughters graduate from the university. Just the other day, the daughter of one of our original drivers, Anya Zargachuk was by the office to celebrate her 19th birthday. She works part-time at Willard while going to the university. Her father, Sasha, worked for the company more than 15 years. Over the years, you do become a family. In fact, I married one of the original cast, but we divorced, and she moved on.

After my little speech, Mako asked me to go to lunch with him. At the time, there were only four or five places expats actually went as opposed to the many dozens available today. Ukraine was gray and sullen that first year. Today it wears makeup, sometimes sloppily applied, but still not as gaudy as Moscow.

We went to the National Hotel, a government-run facility that reminded me of a mausoleum. It had a cavernous first floor with the obligatory kiosk selling books and souvenirs. The restaurant, at that time, was Soviet-style, with long tables for groups of people to sit; even if people didn't like or even know one another. I gingerly ordered through a translator what appeared to be safe. We were warned to stay away from leafy vegetables and to drink only bottled water. When I first visited the Soviet Union 25 years earlier, I caught a parasite that hung in there for months, cutting down substantially on my quality of life and range of maneuverability. Today, I sometimes drink from the tap and eat whatever I want, but after so long, the body machine grows accustomed to whatever bacteria invades.

With good intentions, Mako filled me in on some of the cast I had just inherited. I was grateful for the rundown, but from past experience, I equated it with some people like broccoli and other people don't. In other words, I needed to make my own judgments, and would do so in the coming weeks.

Mako zeroed in on a beautiful former model named Natasha Lotra, who headed up the television portion of the education program. "She's a troublemaker," he said. "You'll have to keep an eye on her. She is probably the person in the program closest to Nunn."

Billy Kimbell, the expat television guy, reiterated the Lotra warning when we were at dinner one night, but Kimbell was not to stay with me long. At the same dinner, he said he had no confidence in the future of the program. We were at the Apollo, a nice restaurant in the passage way, just off Khreschatyk Street. He sounded so depressed that I suggested that evening he might want to leave the program and return to the United States. "I have a job to do," I said. "I don't want anyone who is not totally on board." On the cusp of my 50th year, I was Boy Scout gung-ho.

Natasha's television group produced three programs, and I was later to add a fourth. It was American taxpayer dollars at work. For the first time in years, I didn't have to worry about making payroll or in meeting revenue targets set from on high. We also published a weekly newspaper, and had two radio programs, not to mention we fielded a regional apparatus of six offices spread across the country.

For a fellow like me who had struggled in the West Virginia economy, it was all-day recess where they handed out lollipops, tutti frutti and huge yellow dollops of my favorite banana pudding. Not having to worry about making a payroll was a huge relief.

It all was to support the mass privatization effort, a commendable but partly misplaced effort. It was courtesy of the U.S. Government, and it was smoother than any money-laundering scheme ever devised, though the funding agency never envisioned it as such. The government – ours in partnership with the Ukrainian one – was cleaning not money but huge and generally inefficient enterprises. Both governments were well-intentioned; they just didn't realize the eventual outcome. Or maybe they did.

It worked like this:

The government printed privatization certificates for every man, woman and child in Ukraine. We ran an educational program on the benefits of a market economy and urged everyone to pick up their certificates, which generally were free, though in certain districts people made money off them. The theory was that the common folk would invest those certificates in a local factory or plant, and someday, if that particular company did not go bankrupt, there might possibly be a return on that little investment. They were, in essence, getting a piece of the rock – not a big piece, just a sliver. However, there was one hitch to spreading the wealth: Investment companies sprang up and bought the certificates from the little guy for a song, and then took over huge enterprises in minerals, foods, paper products – everything from giant steel mills to companies that made wire clothes hangers. There was nothing illegal about this. The people who were smart enough and had the resources to do this were later called oligarchs because most also managed to hold down posts in Ukraine's legislative branch, the parliament (the Verkhovna Rada). They became billionaires, drove around in Maybachs with window curtains, and paled around with former U.S. presidents on occasion.

But who could blame them? Boys will be boys. I think we – in this case USAID, the World Bank, Price Waterhouse, and various other funding organizations – were rather naive as to how the program in reality would work. Our goal and that of USAID was to make sure that everyone obtained a privatization certificate, and at this we were largely successful. We all became too involved in the process, and lost sight of original objectives. But we felt at the time we were doing something good and right, that if we were not doing God's work, we were at least missionaries for truth, justice and the American way.

To their credit, the oligarchs finally came to terms with the type people they were, and embarked on campaigns to see who could spend the most money on hospitals, the arts, childhood diseases, AIDS, and any number of redemption projects. One even gave free concerts on Independence Square, bringing in the likes of Elton John and Paul McCartney in an effort to raise money to fight AIDS. They did such a good job, a magazine I published through much of the current decade, *The Ukrainian Observer*, named such philanthropists Ukrainians of the Year. We took a good bit of flak over this, but several years later I still believe it was a good idea. One decade's robber baron is today's name on a library or medical wing.

To my knowledge, no one ever apologized for the haywire program, that banshee-like rush to mark off a checklist. It was mission accomplished, but at what price? It was a very sloppy privatization where wealth was not distributed but held by the very few who were smart enough, and aggressive enough, to see opportunity in the folly of the program. I think we all made the wrong turn somewhere, and could have done a much better job in the years following independence.

But, to a larger extent, the education program I headed was just that, about education and not pushing privatization certificates as if they were little White Castle hamburgers, though, in truth, that's about what they were worth to ordinary Igors and Ivans. Two greasy sliders, coming up.

Our program's success was measured by the percentage of people who picked up certificates, which, as I recall, was about 80 per cent. This wasn't bad considering that we only had about a year and less than $7 million.

Chapter
6

My Kingdom

When we returned from lunch at The National, Bill Mako went back to his side of Dom Kino, and I sat in the office with the big, black conference table, surveying my new kingdom. Nunn had bought serviceable furniture for the program, and had made the director's office one in which he could see out but others could not see in. The remainder of the office was everyone else, bullpen style, with the exception of the design studio, which was in a separate area. David Payne, who had not arrived yet from his few days in Russia, was the advisor for the design group.

I hardly emerged for a week. I closeted myself in that office and did some serious thinking. There were two trains of thought: 1) If I were to make this education program a success, I had to direct it toward the goal, and not just produce tangential television and radio programs, or publish newspapers and other publications. There were no clearly defined messages. Most everything appeared to revolve around telling success stories and listening to talking heads in government pay lip service to market reform. There were tactics, but no umbrella strategy. The second bit of deliberation had to do with a career challenge. What was I to get out of this experience? For what purpose was I so far away from home?

The first challenge was not that difficult. The people I managed were extremely talented – more than that, they were resourceful. They were also easy to lead. Within the first week, I had worked on detailed strategies and tactics for each department within the program. I had a plan and was now ready to share it, ready to come out of the glass-enclosed office. When I finally did emerge, I learned what the Ukrainians were calling me: "The man in the bubble."

The second train of thought was more introspective. It was the Who am I? question and What the hell am I doing? If I were going to press the pedal to the metal entering my fifth decade, what direction was I to steer? Before coming to Ukraine, I was a cheap country song, the kind some yokel who would never make the big time singing at Tootsie's Orchid Lounge on lower Broadway in Nashville. I had been there. I had tossed back Buds, hunted for a column I had written that was pinned to Tootsie's wall, had sat down with Tootsie who told me Roger Miller wrote "Dang Me" on a paper napkin in that booth, and listened to some would-be Hank Williams sing about a 'tear in my beer." I wanted more. I wanted a rhinestone prairie.

Ukraine represented a real break from the past, a life-defining moment, one of those opportunities that come at you like a Nolan Ryan fast ball; and, if you don't swing and your timing isn't perfect, there will be a whiff and some disembodied voice will yell, "YOU'RE OUT!" That wouldn't be me, I vowed, I would be ready for my moment, and my moment was now.

Working early in the morning before coming to work, I started on a new novel. It was to be a detective story, but more than a potboiler. Something on the order of a Kurt Vonnegut book, a little more cerebral than my previous efforts, that managed never to find publishers. I had already written two books. The first Doubleday said had some promise but was a little too ethereal for commercial consumption. It was called *The Old Man Who Walked So Far* and was an allegorical Christmas story written for my young son. It was meant to be a short story but ended one year and 700 typed pages later. Doubleday said they wanted to see something else from me, and I immediately began work on *Shadow of Doubt*, a blood-spattered horror/detective story. It also took a year and it was another few months before I heard from Doubleday that they liked my first book better. So, I divided my fiction writing into that which was "trash" and "non-trash" as opposed to fiction and non-fiction.

One day in a discussion with my translator about a serious matter of missing items from the education program, Volody Iszotov fingered a possible suspect and said, "A thief wears a burning hat." I immediately had a title for my new non-publishable book. Over the next year, I cranked it out. Though it never found a publisher, the book led me to the more practical route of writing non-fiction books

About that same time, one of our designers, Dima Orlov, heard that I was a wannabe painter, and that I mostly used pastels. He brought me a framed canvas. About the same time, I discovered oils, and found I much preferred the more vibrant colors to the timidity of pastel chalk. Hence, I embarked on a painting spree that has never stopped and the work effort has left 400 plus canvasses in my home, various garages, and even on a few walls. My first exhibition was to be a few years later at the prestigious L-Art Gallery in Kyiv. I sold six paintings and donated the proceeds to a hospital for older Ukrainians.

From age 50 to 60 was a sprint. If I slowed down physically, I sped up mentally. Up until my sixth decade, I was living a life in tactics without a single strategy to sustain and guide me. Most everything that happened to me was simply through happenstance, like fiddlesticks dropping from the sky and accidentally falling into neat rows. I had worked hard all my life, but had also been very lucky. I'm not talking lottery winning lucky; but when things seemed the darkest, or boring, or even too difficult, an opportunity knocked, and there was nothing subtle about it.

When *f*was finished, I embarked on a book about managing crises in Eastern Europe *(Dancing With The Bear)*, having had much practice in the region by then and having been on Burson-Marsteller's crisis simulation team. Then, I completed a very short book on media training *(Accidental Headline)*, making it more a narrative than a manual.

By this time, I had accumulated numerous adventures over a lifetime, and encapsulated them in *The Flak*, a book about my life in public relations. Within reach of my 60th birthday, I wrote what I believed was by far my best book, *The Portfolio Bubble: Surviving Professionally at 60*, a survival book for those who do not aspire to retire. Next came *The Silverback Diaries: The Manager as Hero*, a collection of some of my mostly common-sense but sometimes off the wall management ideas.

Between 50 and 60, I was the Renaissance man, or at least thought I was. I had held two painting exhibitions and had actually sold my work. I had written five books (Silverback came later), and *Portfolio Bubble* had garnered favorable reviews from dozens of sources. The Ukrainian press had covered both my art exhibitions. So, I was riding high on my pony, breathing an air so rarified it smelled like sweet perfume, the kind your first girlfriend wore and which you still remember. It was to come crashing down on me on or near my 60th birthday, when I found that I was not only not invincible, I wasn't that great of a husband and father. But, this is a story for a little later, following a second wife, and when I was well on my way to becoming what I jokingly refer to as a serial marriage-er.

When I finally emerged from the bubble office, I had been to the mountaintop and back, both professionally and personally. I had a strategy for the education program, and we were going to focus on it like a laser beam. We were going to preach the gospel of market reform, and make it stick. We were going to make a skeptical audience forget 70 years of Communism as if it were a bad relative that came to dinner and simply stayed too long. Along the way, I was going to make tons of money for my company and a little for myself.

Part of this strategy had to do with gaining the confidence of the Ukrainian team. To them, I was an unknown commodity. I was the guy brought in when they were perfectly satisfied with the previous guy. They didn't see the logic in changing directors.

Within the month, Nunn made it to the third floor of the Dom Kino building. He was a full-of-energy-and-ideas Englishman, the type fellow who exudes confidence He had been awarded another USAID contract and the resources of the education program were to support his efforts. I saw no reason not to attempt to meet his goals and ours at the same time. At that time, I wanted to please everybody. That was to last only a few weeks.

The education program's flagship television program was called "Crossroads" in English. In it, local television personality Alla Mazur interviewed officials involved in the market reform process. There was also an audience, generally made up of employees of the education program. Multiple cameras were used to try and make the program interesting, but there was not a whole lot that could be done with such a one-dimensional product, even if you were to use dozens of cameras, an overhead boom and multiple meters of track along which to move the cameras. It was like watching my grandmother knit a sweater.

I immediately set out to change the program, by altering its vision and scope. I wanted to make it people-oriented and not a suck-up to various officials. I wanted show time, not snooze time. I wanted it to stand for something, and that something was in line with the strategy I had developed. It would be about people, ordinary people, and not just the high and mighty.

Though I had virtually no experience in television, I pretended I was a combination Edward R. Morrow and Cecil B. DeMille with a little John Ford tossed in for good measure. "Crossroads" became not a simple themed program with one interview, but many programs wrapped into nearly an hour of broadcasting. It was a variety show of fast-moving hard news, illustrative soap operas, and "60 Minutes"-style vignettes. It went from being Guy Lombardo to Bruce Springsteen overnight.

But it was not easy. Natasha Lotra, the director of the education program's television department, was not anxious to see the show evolve. In the beginning, she fought the very idea of changing it a little bit. However, I tore the damn thing to pieces and reconfigured it with a whole new set of Tinker Toys. The director of the previous "Crossroads" show had to be benched in favor of younger talent.

About this time, I discovered a young film director, Sasha Itigilov, who was only 20 years old. I put him to work piecing together some of the more hard-hitting investigative pieces as well as some of the more visually interesting shows. The show now had character. It also started to gather an audience.

I have never thought of myself as ruthless. However, I have acted quickly when I have found hurdles in the way of reaching goals. It was easy to recommend that Billy Kimball leave the education program when he said his heart was no longer in it. We parted as friends. Much later, I had to make one of the most difficult decisions of my life, and that was to end a partnership with David Payne, someone I genuinely liked. However, on a late May morning, I did it without hesitation to help save the business and the livelihood of nearly 100 people.

Throughout the early days of the education program, I made winning over Natasha Lotra a goal. It actually had nothing to do with the fact that she was a lovely lady. However, her personality is rather specific. She can be gracious but at times difficult. In 15 years, I have on occasion gone toe-to-toe with her over personal issues. However, we've always made up, if not by the time the sun went down, at least by the end of the week. Also, during difficult times, she has always been supremely loyal.

Though Natasha did not speak English (her English is good now), I met with her often over "Crossroads" and other aspects of her department. We all realized that television, at that time, was the best way to get information into the bloodstream of the Ukrainian consciousness, and that it would be important to the education program for us to reach an agreement on the format of the shows we broadcast. Natasha eventually came around, and became a proponent of and cheerleader for the new direction of "Crossroads".

Natasha was just one of a half dozen Ukrainians who were the real muscle behind the education program. Tania Spiridonova, a willowy blond with grit and determination, headed up the radio department. Roman Diukarev, an Estonian who lived in Moscow, who was later to become my good friend, had brought both Spiridonova and Natasha Lotra on board during the first days of the program. Tania developed into a superb advertising strategist, and was later named president of our advertising company. Natasha eventually became chief operating officer, and continued to supervise our largest account, Philip Morris.

About a dozen of the 75 or so people who were in Dom Kino were with me 15 years later. Most were in leadership positions then and now. Many in the program became entrepreneurs and started their own businesses, of which I am exceedingly proud. If the overall mass privatization program was an effort that perhaps could be held up to question, our people did learn a trade in advertising or public relations; and, perhaps as sad commentary, those professions paid vastly better than did being a doctor or a scientist. While it was not on our USAID "task order", I believe we fulfilled what should have been a primary mission: We eventually privatized the education program.

A Visitor from the U.S.

It was a beautiful September when my world was launched

in Ukraine. Winter, however, was to come early, and it was to be one of the coldest in memory. This is important because my then-wife, Becky, happened to visit that December. It was not the most pleasant time for her to come, and it was the last time she made it to Kyiv. She stayed a month, and it was a long, long month for her.

I had met Becky when she was 18 and I 19 at a junior college in Orlando. She was a reporter on the school newspaper and I was the chief editor. She covered the local fraternity, and I was about to get kicked out of the fraternity due to writing editorials that criticized the organization for being more social than socially responsible. She also was supportive when the private junior college's board of trustees suggested strongly that I leave the school. My transgression was to suggest that they allow blacks to attend. I called their bluff and continued to write that which didn't at all please this uptight and conservative board.

Becky and I dated throughout the year, and then left for the University of Florida together. Two years later we were married, and Kelly came along 10 months later. Rob, who is African-American and Mexican, was adopted when he was two, several years later.

But, of course, one can't blame the weather on a marriage not working any more than you can say a match lit in Kyiv caused a fire in Orlando. Our marriage, in fact, did work. It worked for quarter a century and more, and they were good years, some great years. Time just ran out on us. We didn't change, but we did evolve.

Becky was more liberal than I when it came to "ships passing in the night" relationships. If it bothered her, she didn't go into histrionics and toss me into the street. Hence, there were a few incidents, and those were far between. While not an ideal husband, I wasn't a serial philanderer and this in itself was a little abnormal for a newspaper reporter who came of age in the late 60s and early 70s. However, after one incident, she packed condoms in my suitcase when I went off on my next trip. I didn't dare open them, though.

I have found over the years that men play around with women not nearly as good looking as their wives. That was certainly the situation in my case. As the old commercial went, Becky never got older, she just got better. In the end, I messed up. Becky understood an occasional dalliance, but not her husband thinking he was in love with another. That was really unforgivable.

In Ukraine and on my own, it was difficult to remain true blue in a land of milk and honey, where the most erroneous impression of Soviet life held by Americans was of a sad-eyed, heavy-set woman, in country calico dress and wearing a bandana over her head. One of the first things I learned on landing in Ukraine was that the women did not look like jovial, obese Nina Khrushchev. Most looked more like Julie Christie in the movie "Dr. Zhivago". Don't get me wrong: There were married expats who came to Ukraine alone, and I am sure were totally faithful. I just never met many.

Chapter
7

A Place Apart

In 1994, Kyiv was not the Kyiv of today, or even the Kyiv of six years later. It still held longingly to its communist past, and its denizens walked unsmiling down Khreschatyk, the short but main street that bisects the two sides of the capital city. That is what I remembered most vividly in those early days, sadness.

Some evenings, I would walk through the underground passageways that crisscrossed beneath Khreschatyk, a place where women sold flowers and cigarettes and served as unofficial moneychangers. Often, a crowd of old and weather-beaten men and women with gray, matted hair, tired, yellow eyes and overcoats that smelled of sausage would gather and sing songs about how it use to be. Later, market reform would change many lives, but not these lives. At the time, the World Health Organization listed the average length of life of the Ukrainian male as 60. They succumbed to too much alcohol, a medical system that was falling apart, and a safety and environmental climate that was dismal.

At that time, expatriates ran in packs, like wolves. They partied together; they shared apartments, ate together, and, on occasion, they slept together. There were a few lone wolves, including me. However, I was older, and that which appealed to a 20-something didn't appeal that much to a fellow sliding into 50. I liked a solitary barstool at the Dnipro Hotel, and didn't mind fending off the aging prostitutes that offered up solicitation lines as subtle as a death screech in an opera's final act. The Ukrainians called such ladies "night butterflies". It was all grist for the book I had just undertaken.

My routine was pretty much the same each day. A driver – my first was Igor Panchenko, who is now our web developer – would pick me up early from my apartment just off Mikhaylivska and, as usual, I was always the first to arrive in the office. About an hour later, a few others would trickle in, and an hour later a few more. In the beginning, I did my best to enforce a 9 a.m. starting time.

However, Ukrainian body clocks generally run on a totally different time than mine. Eventually, years later, I capitulated but in a way I felt was inventive. I developed the 24-hour workday and said come in at whatever time that pleased you, but put in a good eight hours. They could even divide it into sections if they wished. There was also a realization that many of the women who worked in the program and later at Willard had young children and, in some cases, less ambitious husbands. In other words, they had to buy nappies and groceries while the would-be hunter-gatherer was busy playing fighter pilot computer games.

I would normally leave around 7:30 p.m., after it was dark. That's what made it a little gloomy; coming to work while it was dark and leaving when it was dark in the long winter months. Igor would drop me off at Apollo in the Passage, where I would sit at the bar and have my dinner. One night it would be spaghetti Bolognese, and another what could reasonably be described as steak, but tough as leather. Normally, there were few other customers, though occasionally the same gangster would come in and eat alone, while his two bodyguards watched. He wore a silk suit, while they wore Nike-branded running outfits. This particular gangster was to become a central figure in the novel I was writing. While a creature of habit, I went to the Apollo because the people were nice and they had English-language magazines, though at an exorbitant price. It was also only a 10-minute walk from my home.

One drizzly night while returning to Dom Kino from a meeting at the State Property Fund, I heard a series of shots as I was about to open the door to the building. There was a huge ruckus that looked in the dark almost like a Rugby scrum. Curious, I looked on. When the group finally broke up, two men lay dead on the ground in the middle of the street. This was a common occurrence during this period. The gun or the bomb often settled arguments. In Eastern Ukraine, a bomb exploded in a football stadium killing its intended targets, but also, blowing away the Ukrainian equivalent of a hotdog vendor. In that same city, Donetsk, a local oligarch got off a plane with his wife, and gunmen drove onto the tarmac and gunned both of them down. Maybe this is the reason we were given our generous $101 a day per diem. In any event, all the mayhem in Kyiv, Moscow and elsewhere was what gave rise to the term the Wild East, which, for a while, was not an exaggeration.

There were a limited number of expat hangouts, and these were places many Ukrainians simply could not afford. One where there was a mix of expats and Ukrainians, however, was Karambol, a pool hall with a painting of a giant rooster on the outside wall. For a while, it drew expats like a magnet, but that didn't last. We expatriates were fickle consumers. It was very crowded, and often on weekends only a bribe to the staff could get you a game. Because billiards was my sport, I spent many nights there. For several years, I had a Gandy Savannah pool table in a room of my Charleston home, and practiced daily. That is not to say I was good, merely slightly better than average, but that was good enough to generally win.

I had been in Kyiv about eight months when the Studio opened, and the new restaurant was immediately elevated to icon status. What with its pictures of Marilyn Monroe in various poses and its stainless steel tables, it was one of the first restaurants to totally abandon any semblance of Ukrainian décor or any nod toward early bordello, which characterized the Apollo. It was located around the corner from the Dnipro Hotel at the end of a passageway. Today, it is home to the Grand Café. It became the scene of many expat going-away parties, a ritual which became more frequent as different Western government programs, including the education program, cut back.

My first expatriate recruit in those early months was Karen Diakun, who had been responsible for new business in Burson-Marsteller's Washington office. She was Ukrainian Diaspora without the affectations of Ukrainian Diaspora. For starters, she hadn't gone to Ukrainian schools in the U.S. and didn't speak the language. She was Slavic pretty, and had the drive of the Energizer Bunny. She was the first of seven expats to join the program over a near two-year period. Burson-Marsteller made money on the number of expats in country, as well as on the individual Ukrainians. Each were assigned a value somewhat above their salary. I was probably the only expat the company lost money on in that my salary was greater than the government day rate awarded the company. However, I effectively managed the others, and made money for the company at every opportunity.

In short order, we also brought in Glenn Sapadin, a hugely likeable Jewish fellow from New York; Jason Penchoff, who had been my personal assistant in Washington and first mate on the *Kelly Dawn*; Patty McDonough, a Burson staffer who loved funky hats, and Nazan Armenian, an exotic woman with a terrific personality who had been Kirby's assistant in Washington. Also on the list was Deborah Plumstead who to this day continues the expat life, working for a public relations company in Dubai. There were also a few forgettable clunkers. One American, hired by Kyra Cheremeteff sight unseen, came in from Poland. He was the only person I actually tossed out, eliminated, so to speak, with extreme prejudice. Other than being a masher, his most deadly sin was referring to Ukrainians as "these people" and "this is not the way we do it in a civilized country." I don't even remember his name.

With each expat, I took them aside and gave them the same, almost fatherly lecture. "You are a guest in this country and never forget it," I would begin. Eventually I got around to giving them the most important advice. "You think you can drink. You're nothing compared to these guys. If you try to out-drink them, you will be embarrassed."

Kyra also brought on board Myron Wasylyk, who worked for us at the State Property Fund as an American advisor to the chairman. He was the only one among us who could speak fluent Ukrainian, other than Peter Bejger, who advised on publications. Myron had worked in the first Bush administration at a mid-level position that, having been the Senate leader's go-to guy, did not impress me. However, Myron later became a worthy competitor with another company, PBN. When it came time to "privatize" the education program, and start Burson's first commercial office in Ukraine, Myron was not one of the 25 people I selected from the program. However, I should have. He was immediately picked up by PBN, which inherited the fading remnants of the USAID sponsored program, and now Myron effectively manages the PBN Kyiv office.

I was closest to those expats who had come via Burson-Marsteller. It seems we had more in common. This is particularly true of Jason, Patty, Nazan and Karen, who all had held previous jobs at Burson. However, while Sapadin never worked at Burson, he fit well into the group. I think there was some kinetic happening that threw us all together, an alchemy of something right and good. What socializing I did, I did with them, but being much older I had an excuse to leave early. I tended to start saying goodbyes by 9 p.m., anxious to get on to priorities that I didn't consider when I was their age, like writing books and painting. They often partied through the evening. I admired that, but couldn't do it.

In early spring that first year, we all took to the Dnipro River with a vengeance. I rented a boat and a captain for the summer, paying at that time just a few hundred dollars. My boat – in fact most all boats – looked like props from a Mel Gibson Mad Max movie. They were made of metal and most were homemade. Mine was about a 25-footer with a cutty cabin. We would putt-putt up or down the river, find a good spot on one of the many islands, and glide to a stop through the sandy river bottom. We would immediately begin foraging for dried wood for shashlyk or barbeque. Invariably, someone would bring a guitar and commence strumming while others took a cool dip in the river. Having not taken my shirt off since 1954 – a slight exaggeration – I was content to watch from the bank. But the fact is, at that time I was up to 110 kilos, or 242 pounds, and was very self-conscience of my weight. Looking back, though, this first summer in Ukraine was idyllic, a gauzy, nearly slo-mo 50-millimeter experience.

There was something else that made it interesting: a raven-haired lady named Tanya who was in the regional department of the program. In the meetings I had with regional, I had eyed her from time to time, thinking she looked more mature than her 29 years. At the time, I also learned that she was involved with another Ukrainian in the regional group.

I had no driver on weekends, but I found myself walking to work to see whether, by chance, she had decided to put in a few extra hours. I found that most weekends she was there, and I would walk over to her desk and say a few words of encouragement that she didn't understand. Her knowledge of English was less than basic, but she communicated very well with her eyes, and I could tell there was a flicker of attraction.

I had my 50th birthday that first May in Ukraine, and I decided to go with Ukrainian custom and throw myself a party. However, it wasn't to be just any party, but an evening cruise on a sizeable boat for 150 or so of my closest friends. This was interesting in that my close friends probably numbered less than five or six. Everybody likes a party though, and the one marking not only my birthday but Victory Day in Eastern Europe, May 9, 1945, seemed to give impetus to the affair. There was a Dixieland band, a very large cake, and enough booze to fill the Black Sea, or so it seemed.

During the cruise, I danced with many ladies, both on the boat and when we stopped for shashlyk. For some reason, I ended up holding hands in the darkness with Tanya, or, at least I think I did. Everyone had had a lot to drink. By the time we docked, I had been given enough flowers to put an oligarch's funeral to shame. As I recall, the van driving the band took me back to my apartment and unloaded all the flowers and presents. There was something sad about the moment. There I was, all alone, having turned 50, the sweet fragrance of dozens and dozens of flowers scattered throughout my living room, and no one with whom to share the moment. I went to bed very alone that night. It wasn't to last long, however.

Several weeks later, I was scheduled to make my first trip to Crimea, an autonomous republic of Ukraine, where I was to attend and speak at a press conference in Simferopol and the next day address a group of enterprise managers in Yalta, as well as meet with the head of the local State Property Fund. My media manager, Maxim Rylsky, suggested an assistant in the press department should take the train and arrive early to finalize arrangements. We would follow in two cars.

Where there is opportunity and motive, there is risk and possible reward. "Max," I said, "perhaps we should have someone with more experience do the advance work." I suggested Tanya Tyagur from the regional department. Max seemed a little puzzled, but agreed with the decision.

A brief interruption of narrative here. The fact of life is I have never ignited a serious relationship with someone who did not work with me. This, of course, violates all the human resource rules, and generally suggests disasters waiting to happen. It also conjures up the whole power game. No one has ever hinted harassment, and I tend to bend over backwards in this area, to the point of timidity.

While I am not different from anyone else in pursuing relationships, reaching other goals drives me, and my sphere of social activity rarely extends beyond the workplace, and all the ramifications that go with it. Just as you would not find me at a church social, I have rarely been the type to cruise the local bar scene. Three work-related relationships ended in marriage, one lasted 25 years, another 10 and another I hope the rest of my life. There was another that was a relatively brief, intense affair, but we were, indeed, equal partners in the business. It could be argued that my first marriage was incubated in a pseudo work atmosphere. As noted earlier, I was the editor of the school newspaper, and my future wife a reporter. However, it furthers my argument, so I enter it into evidence. Also, if such statistics are to be believed, 40 per cent of relationships start in the workplace.

Tanya took the train to nowhere, or at least it seemed that way. Throughout the day, we checked on the progress of the southbound choo-choo to Crimea, but it seemed to make little progress. There were breakdowns and slowdowns, and it took nearly 30 hours for her to arrive. We started out by car early the next morning.

By the time Tanya arrived in Simferopol and checked into the hotel, we were pulling up to the front of the hotel. A press officer of the national State Property Fund, Ludmila Vasilyava, and a translator, Volody Izotov, accompanied Max and me. It was a small, well-contained contingent, and it was only my second diplomatic mission, so to speak, on behalf of the education program. While I was being checked in to the hotel, I sat next to Tanya. For some reason, she pulled out her passport and showed me her picture. Her hair was in Ukrainian style braids, and she looked more like a teenage girl. We talked little, and what little communication we did was through furtive glances, and signals that were non-verbal, non-sequiturs. Throughout our relationship, we often misunderstood one another, both from a language and perhaps even a cultural standpoint, like two ships passing in a channel through dense blue fog.

By early afternoon the next day, we had concluded what one could call a successful press conference. I had given a small speech, and answered questions the best I could. My co-speaker on the platform, the local State Property Fund chairman, was later assassinated, which was not an uncommon phenomenon. I never understood the reason, and I am not sure anyone else did either, other than it was somehow related to his business dealings.

That evening at the hotel we had dinner and all in my party gathered later in my two-room suite that had a balcony overlooking nearby hills. We sat around the table offering up toasts for most any occasion, and I related stories about my first trip to the Soviet Union, and meeting with Foreign Minister Andrei Gromyko and other legendary officials. I was the only one at the table, other than Volody the translator, who spoke English.

After a short while, we ended up on the balcony, drinking and talking. I gravitated toward Tanya, and we held hands behind our backs so as not to arouse suspicion. At a certain hour, when all were tired and with a full schedule the next day, everyone left my room, including Tanya. Tanya motioned that she would return.

That evening began a 10-year relationship that resulted in a wonderful daughter, Mia, and my adoption of her daughter, then five, Masha. If I knew then what I know now, that the marriage would have a soap opera ending, and that I would be the poor sap left at the station, I still would have indulged and endured. One cannot put a price tag, emotional or otherwise, on the affection for children, and a period in which I thought we were both happy.

It was really not my intention to go into details of either a first or a second marriage. In many ways, it serves little purpose and stirs a pot that boiled over many years ago. Also, it is not something that serves the present, and someone I care about deeply. However, this is the story that I lived, and the thoughts I had then and now, and to be less than truthful would render these pages not merely dishonest but simply paper waiting for the match. Five years later, I harbor no animosity, and am covered with a blanket of ambivalence. I have Olga to thank for that. She was there to pick up the pieces.

As for Tanya, one evening led to many more, often with her having an English/Russian language dictionary at her side. She slowly began to learn English, and we could carry on limited but long conversations. She would later travel with me to Moscow where Burson-Marsteller asked me to head up both the commercial and the government-funded operations. She also was with me during a triumphant return to Kyiv and the purchase of the Burson-Marsteller office.

One day, seven years later, she wasn't with me anymore. I got over it.

Chapter
8

The Stealth Office

I guess if one could have a dream job it would be to manage a USAID program in which millions of dollars come your way without you having to bring in the first client or having to worry about making payroll.

It helped that the cause seemed worthy, and I had colleagues, both expats and Ukrainians, to whom loyalty was not a word to most but a solemn, unspoken oath. I think that is why 15 years later those same people are in leadership positions in our company.

There have been people who have said Mike Willard could not work for someone else, that he wants always to be his own boss. Horse feathers. Those days with the Market Reform Education Program were among the happiest in my entire life. I was Lawrence of Arabia, but instead of a desert there was a lovely city through which the majestic Dnipro River flowed. It is difficult, even for a mammoth public relations company like Burson-Marsteller, to bridle an employee behind the shrubbery that is Eastern Europe.

I was creatively managing. I was creatively coming up with concepts for television scripts, print ads and I was creatively finding ways to extract those taxpayer dollars from the program and deposit them with Burson-Marsteller. The program was working. After a slow start, people by the thousands began picking up their privatization certificates. Our market philosophy would soon help give rise to a burgeoning middle class.

At the same time, there was accountability for every dollar. It all had to fit within the framework of USAID task orders, and a Price Waterhouse accountant named Charlene Eastin dotted the "i's" and crossed the "t's", while watching the money like a hawk with green eyeshades. But that was okay. I welcomed it. In fact, a few years later several reputable public relations and ad companies were found not to be doing such a good job in terms of stewardship of government money on stateside projects, and people went to jail.

The previous year at Burson I had struggled with devilish timesheets where one had to record to the quarter hour every activity. At my age it sometimes takes that long just to piss or to tie my shoes. I had a first boss, a second boss and then the bosses of all bosses at Burson. In Ukraine, I was lightly tethered to Kirby Jones and Kyra Cherimetiff in Washington, but I got along famously with both. By this time, I was also an executive vice president and position-wise on the same level as Kirby and a notch above Kyra. However, we worked as a team regardless of the positions we held. It was not something we thought about.

In fact, the only time Kirby ever got nervous was after had we launched the stealth office, the little Burson-Marsteller outpost in Kyiv, which somehow, someway, flew under Tom Bell's radar. Tom was the CEO at the New York headquarters, and was rather astonished when he found he now had a 25 person-and-growing commercial office in Ukraine. His philosophy was fewer offices, not more.

I remember shortly after the war in Bosnia in 1996 being sent on a temporary assignment to give public relations advice to the Bosnian prime minister on certain issues unresolved by the Dayton Peace Accords of the previous year. Though hostilities had ended, there was still danger from landmines. As our plane approached the airport at Sarajevo, we were advised to sit on our flak jackets because sometimes there was firing from below. However, it was an uneventful landing on a United Nations plane, and we hopped into a waiting taxi.

One evening I was in the incongruent situation of watching Larry King on CNN from a room in which a section had been completely destroyed in the war. I received a call from Kirby complaining of a rather large telephone bill from his newly created Kyiv office. After explaining that it was actually two months' of telephone bills, I said, "Kirby, relax. The Kyiv office will not only make its numbers but will help the Emerging Markets practice make its overall number." We did.

It had been a rather difficult struggle to keep the USAID contract. Burson-Marsteller had won the lion's share of these types of contracts throughout Eastern Europe and the Central Asian republics and in Kyiv, all involved felt we had done a good job. However, there was a move afoot in Washington to award more government-funded contracts to smaller, in some cases Ukrainian Diaspora-connected, firms.

We had won two task orders outright, but the second one had merely been extended three months and then extended month-to-month. The uncertainty was growing tiresome. I made the case for Burson both to USAID's Ukraine chief, Greg Huger, and to the chairman of the State Property Fund, Yury Yekhanurov. Huger was following directions from Washington, and the chairman – who later became a friend – had his hands tied as well (As an aside, friendships gained early on generally stuck in Ukraine. Yekhanurov later became deputy prime minister, then prime minister, and, as I write this, he is defense minister of Ukraine.) .

Also during this period, in an excessive burst of over-the-top journalism one would not expect from the *New York Times*, a correspondent ridiculed various Ukrainian USAID programs and focused in on my education program. The writer took it from a point of view that our expat-led program was out of touch with

Ukrainian reality, and based it on a commercial in which an elderly lady said that while market reform was important for her, it was more important for her grandchild. The grandchild appeared at the end of the commercial. *The Times* report illustrated the article with the observation that the Ukrainian lady gave her little narrative from a rocking chair when there are no rocking chairs in Ukraine. It was an attempt to make our information program look silly. However, the reporter was wrong on two counts: Of course there were plenty of rocking chairs in Ukraine, but also, on review of the commercial, the elderly actress was not even in a rocking chair.

What to do in the face of losing most of our revenue? With Kirby and Kyra, we became inventive.

We had the remnants of another, small USAID social program that Karen Diakun, by then my deputy, was leading, and Burson-Marsteller was about to be awarded a large U.S. Treasury contract to promote the look of the new U.S. currency in Russia and Ukraine. So, for a few months, we had a launching pad for a commercial office, even though both those projects were government funded and would expire within months.

With our involvement in the market reform education program coming to an end after nearly two years, I informed USAID's Huger that I would be privatizing the program. In other words, I was about to take the 25 best people in the program and put them to work for Burson-Marsteller in the commercial realm. Huger was furious, though rather diplomatic. He asked to speak to the Ukrainian leadership of the various education program departments, and came to Dom Kino and my office to do it.

"But Greg," I said, "Isn't this what it's all about? Leading Ukrainians to the market and not have them bound forever to government programs?" I had previously spun off part of our television production group, which later became the private company Delta Television.

Greg still wanted to try and convince the team to stay together and met with my leadership. It was not a successful meeting. All of the department heads took up leadership positions in the new Burson-Marsteller office. While many still remain with me, others have gone on to prominent positions in other companies, and some have started their own companies. I am proud of the graduating class of Burson-Marsteller, which later became The Willard Group that later became simply Willard.

In my view, USAID's attitude typified the shortsighted thinking of such organizations. They get so tied up in the mechanics of a program they forget the larger purpose. They become the business, and forget that they are not really a business at all, but an incubator for businesses and non-government organizations. They help organizations learn to crawl – a worthy objective. But after that, few organizations need walk. While the education program was greatly diminished over the years, it was still alive in some form a decade later. A bullet should have been put into it after the first two years. It had gone from being a trainer to being an enabler and surely a waste of money.

Deciding whom to take into the new commercial office was not easy. Over 20 months I had become attached to most all of them, including a 70-year-old professor, Dr. Vladimir Senchenko. The professor spoke not a word of English and couldn't or wouldn't learn to use a computer. However, he was a walking, talking encyclopedia with a historical knowledge of most everything, dating back to the 1930s famine when he luckily escaped being a hungry family's meal. He was a keeper.

In all, close to 75 people in Kyiv worked with the education program in some fashion, and at that time I didn't know how long a future it had. I started with the heads of the different departments, from media to television, from regional to radio and design. As for expats, we were still working on the Treasury program that was headed up by my former assistant, Jason Penchoff, as well as the social assistance program led by Karen. Peter Bejier also worked on the social assistance program.

However, when it came to the second tier, this was much more difficult. While my future wife Tanya was not a leader of the regional department – the professor was – she worked harder than most anyone, and had demonstrated leadership abilities throughout the education program. She was brought to the commercial operation, and no one, to my knowledge, raised a question as to whether it was proper or not.

I knew I could not afford too many expats, and settled for David as director of advertising; and a new finance director that came aboard toward the end of the education program, Phil Ash, who was a certified public accountant and worked well with the Ukrainian financial team. With the new venture, I knew I was going to have to have a good money guy. Phil had another good quality; he was entrepreneurial and not simply a green eyeshades type. Later, when the social assistance program ended, I brought Bejger over. Peter was also to edit the first editions of the online publication, *The Ukrainian Observer*, we were to start several years later.

While the funds from the Treasury program and a winding-down social assistance program made for a great cushion, I insisted on keeping a separate accounting of the strictly commercial business. I figured we were six months away from both programs disappearing, and we needed to make the new B-M office an entrepreneurial venture. The Moscow Burson-Marsteller office had a similar situation at the time, and made the mistake of living comfortably off funded work. When I took over Moscow's commercial office later in 2006, we had to nearly double the revenue to make a little profit.

We launched the new B-M office in a nondescript building on Dimitrova Street, above a saloon and a grocery store. It had two big open rooms with a small private office for me. Within two weeks of settling in, a car drove-up, several thugs got out, and took the grocery store manager for a ride. He came back rather disheveled, but not noticeably worse for the experience. However, I imagine he got the message, whatever the message was the thugs were delivering.

During this time, it was a common practice to pay a krisha, or "roof", for protection. We were not immune to this and most always paid in a hidden fee through our rent. This allowed us to nominally say we did not pay for protection, but in some form or another, virtually everyone did in the mid-90s.

Additionally, custom had it that you needed a security guard in combat fatigues and packing heat outside your door at all times, including evenings. However, in the entire time I have had or led a commercial business in Ukraine, no security guard has ever had to come to my rescue or the assistance of staff. They were helpful for a few heavy lifting projects or answering a telephone at night. After a while, I insisted that they wear suits. I wanted them to look respectable for our visiting clients.

On one occasion, an angry landlord of one of our employees burst into my office, and was using rather agitated body language in insisting that my employee owed him money. The security guard just stood there, arms folded, looking fierce, but not doing a thing.

Our landlord on Dimitrova, an American, was himself quite the entrepreneur – up to a point. He was one of the main investors in what became known as the Cowboy Bar. He pitched his lot with Chechens and later found out he was being pushed out of the deal when he ordered a drink in his own bar and had to pay for it. He quickly left to go back to the States.

In the beginning, the world was indeed our oyster. Anyone walking down Khreschatyk wearing a suit in those days could pick up new business. For the most part, the major advertising and PR companies were a year or so away from entering the market, and we won business that would normally go to another network agency.

We were, in fact, a network agency. Young & Rubicam, the advertising giant, owned Burson-Marsteller, and starting out our business was about 75 per cent advertising and 25 per cent public relations. Both Philip Morris and Kraft did business with Y&R. They became our anchor clients, along with the communications company UTEL and Sony.

It was during this period, that a fellow named Johan Boden walked through the door on a Saturday morning carrying a little dog. He represented a company called South Foods with agricultural holdings in the rich soil of the Kherson region. The Swedish group he represented wanted to launch a series of condiment products, and his thinking was that Polkovnik ("Colonel" in Russian) would be a good name, sort of like a Ukrainian Col. Sanders of Kentucky Fried Chicken. We huddled with our Ukrainian staff on Monday, and they came up with several alternative names. Just following independence, the feeling was that Polkovnik would not be suitable. It had a musty sound to it, and harkened back to the Soviet period. A young art director, Dima Orlov, offered as an alternative the name Chumak. The Chumaks were the salt merchants of old who traveled in horse-drawn wagons selling salt and other provisions across Ukraine. We put the name into research, and it came out a winner. Today, 12 years later, Chumak is one of Ukraine's most famous brands.

I am quick to note that we had to win both Philip Morris and Kraft. While we represented Y&R in Ukraine, we received very little support from them and had to prove ourselves with the multinationals. We were a network agency in name only. Years later, Y&R lost most of its Philip Morris business and all of its Kraft business, though we – by then Willard – were able to keep much of the business with the two companies.

My role in those early days of Burson's first commercial office in Ukraine was simply to make the numbers for Kirby's Emerging Market Practice, which consisted of a fast-diminishing government-funded business and the Ukrainian commercial office. At the time, I was also putting the finishing touches on *The Thief Wears a Burning Hat*, and was contemplating another novel. It simply wasn't that difficult to make money back then.

However, Kirby was under the gun because the office simply was not supposed to exist. We were, indeed, the stealth office. In fact, CEO Tom Bell's philosophy was that offices cost a lot of money and the fewer the better. He felt a few offices could control and serve large regions. Two years later, he was to spin off not just the Ukraine office, but also the Prague, Warsaw and Budapest offices. Moscow imploded for Burson-Marsteller during the financial crisis of 1998.

Bell had also introduced the "practice" system into Burson-Marsteller, whereby country boundaries are merged and professional staff were centered around practices, such as technology, health, financial, corporate, public affairs and marketing. This diminished the role of the country manager, but he or she was generally given the role of market leader. The market leader actually became more a mentor than a leader. In such a system, the client leader is king. This formula worked, I believe, in the United States, where there are just a few offices for an entire continent. However, it was more difficult in Europe, where each of many countries had generally a single office.

Having run my own business and a business for Burson-Marsteller, I felt the buck had to stop somewhere when it came to who's ultimately responsible for revenue. In many ways, the practice system made a lot of sense, and had certainly gained credence in companies in various international consultancies. Additionally, I wasn't worried about the erosion of power. The system just didn't seem to work very well in

Europe; and was, in fact, dropped within two years. The practices remained, but also so did a strong management office structure.

Another innovation from Bell was to define Burson-Marsteller as a "perception management" company. That was sort of like being defined as a "propaganda" company, a word that previously was a fine descriptor but became something more sinister in the 20th century. This drove me up the proverbial wall.

To me, it was like saying that we don't solve problems, we just manage image. Image is over-rated. Image is fried air. I never went for the old saw that "perception is reality". That's hogwash. In my view, reality is always reality in the long run, and you had better get used to it. If a company concentrates solely on image at the expense of solving fundamental problems, the chances are great that a Mack truck full of hurt will be dumped on the slick PR company.

It sounds as though I thought Tom Bell was a lousy CEO. He wasn't. He was innovative and he shook up the organization. Also, as will be foretold later, he is the person most responsible for a company called Willard. A Tennessean who had worked for former Congressman Robin Beard and one-time Sen. Bill Brock, Bell and I had a lot in common. I had even covered both politicians when I was with United Press International in Nashville. Interestingly, Bell is one of those unique talents who never graduated from college, but still survived and thrived. He went into politics early, and then shined in every position he held. Today, he is CEO of the giant Cousins real estate firm in Atlanta.

As brilliant as he was, however, Tom never anticipated Kirby, Kyra and Willard's stealth office in Ukraine. I think today he would be proud of the creation he never approved.

Chapter
9

Moscow Bound

With the newly formed Burson-Marsteller Kyiv office starting to jell, I had no intention of leaving that which I had just formed, the embryo of what was later to become my own company. Then, there was a call late one night. It was to profoundly change my comfortable life, and not necessarily for the better.

It wasn't merely a call, but more an intense lobbying effort by someone I had met in Washington briefly and who had been hired by Kirby Jones for the Emerging Markets practice. His name was Mark D'Anastasio, and, given what followed, I have absolutely nothing good to say about him.

That first phone call led to many others. Mark began an almost nightly campaign to recruit me for the Emerging Markets practice in Moscow with the promise that I would head up the operation, as well as B-M's commercial operation in Russia. At the same time, I would continue to give overall leadership to the Ukraine operation. It was quite an ambitious portfolio, and the type of personal advancement about which I would normally dream – but perhaps a year earlier. I was fairly well settled in Kyiv. I had started believing my own hype that it was the Paris of the East.

It was clear, on one level, why Mark, who had somehow maneuvered himself into a key position with Kirby and Kyra, wanted me: I had succeeded. The company had achieved strong financial results in Ukraine with the USAID program, the U.S.

Treasury contract and the social assistance work, and now was off to a fast start as a commercial operation. However, in Mark's mind, I represented competition. Or, perhaps he merely adhered closely to the adage of keeping your friends close but your enemies closer, though I did not consider him an adversary at that time.

There were clues as obvious and bold as a Kandinsky painting that should have steered me clear of Mark, Moscow and a change in life at a very inopportune time. At a meeting in New York, I was part of a group grope to bring the Emerging Markets practice together as a cohesive team. There had been a verbal slugfest from Washington to Almaty. It became clear during the meeting, moderated by the late Geoff Nightingale, that Mark was the main reason for discord within the practice. By this time, it seemed no one really liked him. Not really knowing him, I was neutral.

I was flattered by the opportunity Mark offered. If what Mark was saying proved true, it would be a career-building job, and few people at my age (then 51) are afforded such opportunities. I would be leading what could be one of the company's most important offices as Russia moved away from 70 years of communism to a burgeoning market economy, one which had been fuel-injected by an influx of giant multinationals and high oil prices. I felt it could even lead to a bigger job in London or New York. As noted earlier, while I enjoyed my nearly 10 years as an entrepreneur in West Virginia, I was rather happy in the bosom of a giant company.

I discussed the matter with Kirby, who felt it would be a good move for me. If I made Kirby look good in Ukraine, there was a good possibility I would repeat this in a larger pond. The government-funded work reported to Kirby and the commercial work to the European president of Burson, Ferdinand de Bakker.

It would, however, mean leaving Tanya in Ukraine. I told her I would be flying back regularly as market leader for both Russia and Ukraine. That was not good enough. She said she would follow me.

This would be difficult, for in the beginning it would mean leaving her daughter with her parents in Kyiv. For political and other reasons, it also soon became evident I could not offer her a job with Burson-Marsteller in Moscow, even though she worked for Burson in Kyiv.

We found a place to live in the Patriarch's Pond section of Moscow, a hundred meters from Tverskaya Street, the main thoroughfare leading up to the Kremlin, and a stone's throw behind the American Skylight Diner. It was a one bedroom apartment but with a formal dining room where I could set up a small painting studio. Tanya set up a little office for herself on the kitchen table. It came with a rather modest – for Moscow – price tag of $3,000 a month.

From the very beginning, there was trouble in River City. My first meeting with Mark – maybe even the second – went fine. But by the third, it was clear that we disagreed on virtually everything. Mostly, however, we disagreed on the very purpose to which I had agreed to come to Moscow. He seemed to forget that I would still have Ukraine responsibilities, and that I also had a role to play in the commercial operation in Moscow, which, at the time, was bringing in about half the revenue it needed to be viable. In fact, Mark even seemed to resent me having a leadership role in the government-sponsored work in Moscow.

After a while, it became clear that I was merely a trophy, and a tarnished one at that. Mark would be able to say that he recruited Willard for Moscow, but that he was really overrated. I found myself leaving the Emerging Markets office, near the Kremlin, and spending more time becoming acquainted with the commercial operation that was located on the ninth floor of the World Trade Center.

During this time, D'Anastasio constantly criticized Kirby Jones, belittling him as a poor leader who spent most of his time following baseball statistics. He forgot that I had worked next door to Kirby for a year in Washington, and had huge admiration for him, as well as for his No. 2, Kyra Cheremeteff. I looked forward to the times Mark would leave for Washington, where he was based, and dreaded his return.

Also, given the politics, there was no way I could put Tanya to work either on a funded project or with the commercial office, and, as a Ukrainian in Russia, it would be difficult for her to find a professional position outside these opportunities. She had a hard time understanding this.

The atmosphere in the commercial operation was like night and day from the funded work. Even though it lacked the necessary volume of business, the people were talented and I felt that with more focus it could be a great office. Jennifer Gallenkamp, a former American Foreign Service Officer, and Roman Diukarev, a veteran public relations specialist from Estonia, were leading the commercial operation at the time. Both were more than capable. A few years later, Jennifer became head of corporate affairs at Nestle in Moscow and Roman, after a stint as a freelancer, was brought on by Willard to open and manage the Moscow office. He was later named president of public relations for Russia, Ukraine and Turkey. In 2010, as we were being partially acquired by All About Brands of London, I made him a minority partner with an opportunity to share in the rewards if we were to go public in a couple of years.

I had come to Moscow in the dead of winter, shortly after January 1, 1997. At this time of year, Moscow can look like the metropolis from the more darkly filmed Batman movies. There seemed always to be snow spitting from the sky. Huge mounds of dirty snow piled up, making navigating by foot difficult. The roads were nearly impassible due to backed-up traffic. Amid all this were brightly lit screens that splashed product advertisements as if to say, "Take this, Mr. Lenin." Moscow had gone from being the drab Communist city of my mid-30s to a dreary, but commercial enterprise. At least that was my first impression as I worked in the offices of the Emerging Markets practice, a stone's toss from the Kremlin.

Tension between Mark and I heated up by the hour. In the beginning, we were in a sort of Cold War standoff. I accompanied him to meetings with Russian officials as we attempted to win a World Bank contract and felt like a fifth wheel, relegated to being a spectator while he cajoled the stone-faced Russians who were on the receiving end of his pitch.

I felt I was the victim of a bait and switch operation, and that the job had virtually nothing to do with the assignment I had discussed with Kirby and had accepted. I found myself more and more seeking refuge in the commercial operation, away from Mark, and making more trips to Kyiv in aging Soviet-era TU-134 aircraft, the ones equipped with ropes to help you escape the cabin in an emergency.

On one particular evening, things became especially heated. In a small room with just the practice's financial director looking on, Mark and I got into a shouting match that went beyond the bounds of professional disagreement and into using nuclear meltdown profanity, words that quite often lead to blows. The next day, I told Kirby I wanted out, that I didn't want to be in the same room with Mark. Our partnership in Eastern Europe had lasted less than three months.

Since I had been named to Burson's European Board of Directors by virtue of being the titular head of Moscow's commercial office, an upcoming board meeting in London came at an opportune time. CEO Tom Bell would be there, and I would take my case to the highest court. Kirby said he was disappointed, but understood. By then, he had become disenchanted with Mark as well.

In London a couple of days later, I told Bell I wanted to devote all my attention to commercial work in Moscow and in Kyiv, and I felt I could make Burson's Moscow operation profitable within the year. Kyiv was already doing well. I questioned the future of the government-funded work, and predicted that it would soon come to an end. It did, but about two years later.

The CEO seemed more concerned, rightly so, about a $700,000 payable Daewoo Motors had with the Kyiv office, mostly for advertising that had, as is the custom in Eastern Europe, been prepaid. Daewoo worldwide was having financial problems and was about to go into bankruptcy. As I write this, I am not sure upon which Delivering Angel I based my answer, but I replied that it was not a bad debt and it would be collected. I called the managing director of Daewoo's Kyiv office nightly from Moscow, and he kept assuring me that the money would be forthcoming. It was-every cent of it-and I breathed a sigh of relief heard around the world.

As to me devoting full attention to commercial work, Bell didn't hesitate in getting approval from the European president, De Bakker. I washed my hands of the government-funded segment and took over a glass cubicle at the World Trade Center.

Once that first bitter winter ended and I was safely ensconced in commercial activity, it was to be a rather enjoyable period in my life. Instead of meeting with Russians who seemed to resent our presence, we were talking face to face with commercial directors that wanted Western standards maintained for their companies. I found myself leading pitch after pitch, and enjoying the chase. We also started winning new business, and our little office went from being the whiny pup of Europe to being a respectable revenue generator.

I would like to take credit for turning around Burson's Moscow office, but it was really a mixture of timing, incredible luck and perhaps, my intensity on putting scores on the board. Also, there was a nucleus of a great team, particularly Diukrev, Gallenkamp and a fellow named Dima Kravchenko. Previously, they had not been sufficiently focused, and seemed to lack confidence. Together we grew revenue by 35 per cent that first year.

Burson's Moscow office had previously not been profitable – ever, except with government-funded work managed out of a separate office and Burson's Moscow's piece of the U.S. Treasury new money introduction. Some of Burson's finest had tried and had failed spectacularly. A year earlier, the Moscow office had also made the mistake of treating the Treasury work as a commercial client. As noted earlier, I put government work aside in Ukraine, and measured success only on commercial activity.

Moscow was also great professional experience. While I had conducted crisis trainings and simulations in the United States, mostly for Motorola, my actual crisis experience was limited to those weekly and devilish issues that plague most clients, and were not up there with product tampering, extortion, espionage accusations, product contamination, yellow press, or other mega-issues not found quite so often in the West. In one situation, the hired general manager of a cable television system posted guards with Kalashnikov rifles, barring the American owners from their own building. In another, handled ably by Diukarev, several Qualcomm employees were accused of spying. Both instances were resolved satisfactorily through negotiations with the cable general manager, and when the Russian government decided our client's employees were not spies. But, there were some anxious moments. All such incidents, however, gave impetus to my first non-fiction book: "Dancing with the Bear: Crisis Management in Eastern Europe."

On the personal side, summer had me traipsing all across Moscow. I had read Peter Massie's 800-page tome "Peter the Great" and spent many hours on weekends with a guide following the czar's 16th century footsteps. Though my knowledge was dated 400 years earlier, I had more of a familiarity with Moscow than some of the everyday Igors and Natashas who lived in the historic neighborhoods. They thought of Lefortova as a section of the city that contained a prison by the same name. I thought of it from the standpoint of Francis Lefort, the Swiss general and the Tsar's close friend. I also loved to pick a bench around Patriarch's Pond, within sight of Mikhail Bulgakov's home, where he wrote *Master and Margarita*, and wonder and read some more.

I spent hours in the Pushkin Museum, with its great collection of Van Gogh, Matisse, Chagall, and Monet paintings. It was rarely so crowded you couldn't stand in front of a single painting for long moments and study the texture and almost smell the wheat fields of Arlie and the gentle waters of the Seine. Once into spring, the sun played wonderful, floodlit games with the urban landscape, and that which had been previously drab became delightfully pleasing.

It was, in fact, a very good period for me. I painted dozens of canvasses as I broadened my artistic adventures. Relationship-wise, there were no dramas to foretell future problems. Years later, though, Tanya told me I gazed at Moscow through the prism of my own eyes, not hers.

On the professional front, the Burson-Marsteller business was starting to hum. The team had jelled and revenue was growing monthly. A few months earlier, the practice chair, located in Milan, had set what was first thought to be an impossible goal for us to achieve. We were to surpass it. Though I could hear Mark D'Anastasio's footsteps in the distance, he was out of sight and out of mind.

I could almost feel my star rising, though I could not ascertain the trajectory or, indeed, tell if it might be in essence a shooting star and quickly extinguished.

Chapter
10

Then, The Other Shoe Dropped

In the back of my mind, I guess I knew everything was going a little too well. I was not the Maytag repairman who grew bored because the darned machines never broke down, but I feared becoming him.

I often had to tinker with my career, sometimes jump-starting and at other times manhandling it into a higher gear. My entire work life was notable for zigs and zags, though usually for the better. I generally was incredibly lucky. It was sort of like putting a silver ball into motion in a pinball machine, then not paying any attention as it rolled down the incline. My silver ball tended to light up the board, regardless of what I did. But there was one thing I generally did more than anyone else: I tried harder. Chalk up my hustle to being happily put out to work selling those donuts door-to-door at age 12.

All my life, I have seen work as a marathon and not a sprint. Though I have taken chances, I have always believed in the proverbial three yards and a cloud of dust. While life is definitely short, there is sufficient time to grind it out if you have a goal in mind. I always set goals for myself, both personal and work-related, even if I didn't have an overall strategy for reaching them. I always tried to see the openings when they would come and then made a few dramatic career choices. In doing so, I rarely looked back.

I felt workaholics were bores and suck-ups, but at the same time I generally put in a minimum 12 hours a day. However, I didn't measure worth by time. I measured worth and value by what was accomplished. In my life, I have known many people who put in long hours, but failed to do a day's work. I would rather someone spend less time at the office, but – at the end of the day – have more to show for it than the so-called workaholic.

This is the way it has been ever since I can remember. When I worked the early shift for United Press International as a reporter, coming in at 4:30 a.m., I left work at the usual quitting time of 1:30. But I didn't go home. I spent the afternoon interviewing various people either for my weekly column on country music or for a feature story I was working on. My job has rarely, if ever, been work. It has simply been paid time.

But then one day it seemed my luck had run out. While traveling in Ukraine, I received a call that CEO Tom Bell was looking for me, and wanted me to come to London to meet with him. It was rather mysterious, and the secretary who called didn't hint at the reason I was being summoned. I had no reason to feel trouble was brewing, but, at the same time, I was uneasy. It is not everyday that the CEO plucks you from the heart of Eastern Europe for a single meeting in London town.

Over the weekend, I grabbed a flight from Moscow to London's Gatwick Airport, and stayed the evening where I usually do, the Marlborough Hotel in the West End, about a 10-minute walk to the Burson-Marsteller office. The meeting was set fairly early, at 9:30. It was to be in the office of the European president, Ferry De Bakker.

When I walked into Ferry's office, there wasn't only Bell there, but also Ferry, and a former European president and current consultant, Teresa Dorn. Also present was the future head of the European team, Per Heggenes. I knew something serious was about to happen. However, I summoned all the confidence I could, and was as cheerful as one can be when confronted with a denouement I figured was not good. After a few pleasantries, Bell got to the point.

"We need to get our risky markets off the books," he said straight up. "We need to make some decisions on Kyiv and Moscow."

I started the Kyiv office, and it was close to me. In Moscow, I took an office that had never posted a dime's worth of profit, and turned it into a moneymaker. I felt steam rising, and I made a forceful case for both offices to a skeptical audience. But more was going on here. There was a reason for what I felt was madness. Young & Rubicam, Burson's parent company, was going public, and conventional wisdom suggests that any office that has a potential for disaster should be put out to sea – very far out to sea. Both Moscow and Kyiv were considered to be ground zero of risky markets.

My argument was basic. "Together, Russia and Ukraine have about 200 million people. They drink cola, clean their bathrooms and brush their teeth," I argued. "There is a growing consumer class. Now is the absolute wrong time to pull out of either." (At the time, no one was predicting the economic crisis that was to hit the region in August 1998.)

None at the table showed a hand, just the opposite. They were poker faced and politely asked questions for about 20 more minutes before I was excused. Though not intentional, I thought I had made a better case for Moscow than for Kyiv, for multinationals look at the former city as the center of the universe in Eastern Europe. Kyiv was considered a satellite at that time, the city you thought about after having already put a toe in the Wild East, usually in Moscow.

I spent a few more hours at Burson's Bloomsbury Street office, one more night in London, and then headed back to Moscow. On the flight back, I pondered the possibilities. I really wasn't prepared for the eventual outcome, which could have left me without Moscow or Kyiv, and wondering how much the greeters at Wal-Mart get paid.

A few weeks later, Teresa Dorn, the one woman in the London meeting, appeared on my doorstep. Her job was to assess the Moscow office. In essence, her mission was to grade our ability to carry forward with a commercial operation, or should it, in essence, be folded into the government-funded work. For several years, the government program was based in Washington, D.C. and the commercial program had its handlers in London. They had fought one another over just about everything. Having brought the Moscow office to profitability and having led the very profitable funded work in Ukraine, I was incensed that, apparently, I was going to have to compete to keep what I thought was a successful status quo.

I was later to learn that Mark D'Anastasio had, a few days earlier, met with Teresa in Madrid, where she lived. It was Mark's initial, and I admit brilliant, first step toward out-maneuvering a fellow whose business in America's version of the Palace of Versailles – the U.S. Capitol – was to out-hustle as well as out-maneuver. I had been a master on the chessboard of personnel politics and knew how to use my sharp elbows when the occasion called for it.

While Teresa was in Moscow, I set up various meetings for her with our small but growing client list, and I scheduled time for each member of the commercial staff to meet with her. One evening that week, she asked me to dinner at her hotel, The National.

I was confused about the meeting. She was critical of the staff I had inherited but had molded into a winning team. She assessed a director, Jennifer Gallenkamp, and a manager, Roman Diukarev, as being no more than senior associate-level people. These were strong, strategic individuals who would later excel in other positions, as they had in Burson-Marsteller. It was like one of those cannon shots out of the blue that, in essence, becomes the first shot fired in a war. She talked with me in rambling gobbledygook, seeming to ignore our successes and concentrating on the irrefutable fact that I didn't speak Russian. While a personal failing, it had not been a business hindrance. (Several years later when my book *The Flak* was translated into Russian and released as *PRschik*, I was asked at a heavily attended news conference why I didn't speak Russian or Ukrainian after spending years in the region. I replied that I arrived in Ukraine at age 50, and didn't know any expat who learned the language at that middle-age plateau. I started to ask for another question when five hands went up with people who said that they did know someone who had learned after age 50. So, I spent a year taking lessons. I still can't speak Russian, but I can get around.).

The news was to come from Don Cogman, who had been president of Burson-Marsteller Washington when I was there in 1993, and who had since been named chief operating office of the company. We had always gotten along, but his telephone conversation chilled me to the bone, and I wondered if I was having one of those out-of-body experiences, where everything is happening to you but you can't accept that anything is happening to you.

Cogman's words were: "Mike, we are closing Kyiv, but we are going to keep Moscow. We have decided to put Mark D'Anastasio in charge." One of the reasons he cited was that Mark spoke fluent Russian. It was a song that was growing old and very stale.

After the conversation, I left my office cubicle and looked out from the ninth floor of the World Trade Center to the Moscow River down below. "This is not happening," I said. But it was not only happening, it was happening with the force of a runaway freight train.

That afternoon, I told no one of my conversation with Cogman. I felt telling anyone would confirm that it was true. I felt ashamed. There was an *Economist* magazine on my desk, and I instinctively went to the large display ads where universities, large companies and institutions advertised for senior executives. One ad was for a "conflict resolution" manager at the Carter Center in Atlanta, Ga. Sure, why not? I tossed out a letter of interest in a matter of moments (though I never heard back). Nothing else in the magazine seemed that interesting, or, in fact, paid enough to support my growing responsibilities at home and in Moscow or Kyiv or wherever I might land.

Cogman had ended our conversation by saying they would try to find a place for me in Europe. Well, my French was about the same as my Russian, which was as good as my Spanish, which… I didn't have any confidence I would land securely in a European capital. My plane had been shot down, I needed to bail, and I didn't have the slightest idea where I would land. I wasn't even sure if I had a parachute.

In such times, you want the thoughts of people who have been close to you through large chunks of your life. My call was to Gary Auxier. I owed him my position at Burson-Marsteller and, in reality, my one-way ticket to Eastern Europe. We had been one another's mentor since 1974, lived next door to one another in Kentucky, and fished together in the early evening after work. Gary said Cohn and Wolfe, then a Burson-Marsteller subsidiary, was looking for an office head in Atlanta, and he would recommend me.

Within a day, I found that Steve Aiello, the chairman and CEO of C&W, would be in London, and I set up an appointment to meet him for dinner at his hotel. I was on the plane again for London. Originally, I was from Georgia, born in the onion capital of the world, Vidalia. I had many relatives in Georgia, and my brother was an attorney in Atlanta. But, truth was I didn't have a clue about business in Georgia's capital. But then, I didn't know beans about doing business in Eastern Europe three years earlier, and I had been a fairly quick study.

We met at one of those small but fancy hotels in the Mayfair district, the Claridge. I had decamped at my usual, the Marlborough, and taken a taxi to meet with Aiello (who has a more famous brother, actor Danny). We had drinks at the bar and then dinner. I felt the meeting went well, and adjourned to my hotel convinced I had made an impression on the fellow who might be my new boss.

I apparently didn't. The word I got back from Auxier was that Aiello felt I was a little too long in the tooth at 53 to take on such a new assignment; and, anyway, he wanted someone who knew their way around Atlanta's business community. Being from the onion capital apparently wasn't at the top of his list of qualifications. Back to the *Economist* want ads. (Interestingly, the person Aiello chose didn't work out, and the hire resulted in a lawsuit between C&W and the executive he hired. Eventually, it was the beginning of the end for the company's Atlanta office.).

During this time, my monthly pay was sent to my wife in Florida, and I lived off the Moscow per diem and a rather healthy housing allowance. I also was supporting Tanya and helping support her extended family. I needed to find something fast, or else "crash and burn" would be the mildest metaphor for my problems.

A little earlier, I had come across various Charles Handy books on business and life. I had never been someone overly influenced by so-called wisdom put to pulp, and I had never heard a motivational tape that didn't want to make me stick a foot in the sound system. However, Handy's recipe for those in what he called the third stage of life made a lot of sense. He wrote continually about developing talents to put into portfolios.

I took it a step further and came up with my own philosophy, which I labeled Galaxy Thinking. It all had to do with thinking creatively on problems by reaching out to the brightest star (idea), even if at first it seemed incongruent, nonsensical and absolute farce, and bringing it home to roost. To this foundation, I added two other elements: Stealth Timing, which is obvious, and what I called the Ricochet Principle, which relates to political thinking as opposed to blue sky thinking.

Believe me. I know what you are thinking: This fellow who doesn't believe in gobbledygook merely reached into his bag of magic public relations tricks and scooped out the most convenient doggerel. This fellow who doesn't believe in motivational speakers is a wannabe motivator. So be it. In fact several times a year I do speak before business groups, but, to tell the truth, I am much more comfortable on a university campus talking to students, which I do more often.

My thoughts were only later to be chronicled as sections in two books, and the portfolio part was to come much later. However, I started applying my theories (that term would not pass a scientific test) to my own life and my current rather dire situation. The timing was fortuitous, however. It came in a call from David Payne, the fellow who headed up Burson-Marsteller's advertising business in Kyiv.

"Things are not good since you left," he said. "We can't support the business, and Young & Rubicam has turned down our efforts to become a wholly-owned office." David asked if I would come back, at least for a short while, and shore up the situation with Y&R.

Six months earlier, to concentrate more attention on Moscow, I separated myself from the Kyiv office, even gave up my Kyiv apartment in a cost-cutting move for the company. I felt it was time, and I had left a financial director by the name of Shane Hackney in overall charge, backed up by David as head of advertising. However, in a relatively short time, they had lost business, and it appeared that no one, particularly the staff, had confidence the office would succeed. In fact, I was to learn later that several independent small businesses were being run out of the Kyiv office. In other words, everyone was starting to do his and her own thing. I told David I would call him back the next day, but that I had a plan. He didn't know that the office had a limited time to be open, since Burson-Marsteller planned to close it.

Hence, serious Galaxy Thinking.

The next day I sent an e-mail to Burson COO Cogman asking if the company would sell the remnants of the Kyiv office to me. It was a Hail Mary pass because my ability to lay out a substantial amount of cash was minimal. Only a year earlier, the company had invested in the Kyiv office by moving it from the very plain facility over a saloon into a newly renovated and very modern space on Desyatinna, a prestigious area of Kyiv. The renovation had been relatively expensive, and would not have been done if the decision to eventually close had been made just a few months later. From one standpoint, it should have been an easy decision. Burson wanted to rid itself of an office in a risky market, one that had recently been sliding into the red, prior to the parent company going public.

I didn't immediately hear back, but I did receive a note CEO Tom Bell sent to Cogman in response to Cogman's note about me. I was erroneously copied in on it, as sometimes happens. The note read: "Don, this is okay with me if it is okay with you." I figured I had Don's support or he would not have even bothered sending the question on to Bell.

Almost immediately after I received the wayward missive, I received a note from Bell's secretary asking that I disregard the e-mail sent. It was way too late for that, however. I was Kyiv bound.

Chapter

11

Beginning Anew

Within a matter of a couple of days, I was on the Kyiv-bound train, crammed into a cabin with Tanya and Masha, the daughter I was to adopt and who had recently joined us in Moscow. There was another responsibility on the way. We were to name her Mia.

Before leaving Moscow, I had put in a call to my brother Glen, a lawyer and a certified public accountant. Glen was coming off a serious illness a year earlier; about the same time he lost his wife, Carolyn, to cancer. He needed a change of scenery as well as a challenge. Ukraine offered both.

I told him my situation, and asked him if he would be able to help. I needed both financial and legal advice, and I wanted someone with whom I had total trust. You always ask yourself the litmus test question: With whom would I want to share a foxhole? Glen and I don't always see eye-to-eye, but he has always been there for me and I for him. It is easy for some people to misread disagreements we have had from time to time, but that is understandable. We have arguments that some feel have the potential of getting serious. They do, but generally only for a few days.

Glen flew in the day before I arrived, and we met in the morning at a temporary rented apartment. That afternoon, I addressed a shell-shocked staff of about 60, many of whom had written off Burson-Marsteller as not viable in Ukraine, and were just waiting for the buzzards to gather. These were people I knew and liked, but they had no confidence in the current leadership and told me so. I told them I was back to stay, and I was in charge from here on out. It probably wasn't as assertive as Gen. Alexander Haig's "I'm in charge" declaration when President Reagan was shot, but it came close. At least he was somewhere down the Constitutional succession pecking order. I was merely out in left field because I certainly wasn't officially in charge at that time. I just put my head down, marched forward and assumed leadership, knowing full well that leadership can never be assumed; it must be bestowed. I had only been given permission to negotiate to acquire the office.

The financial director, Shane Hackney, a Texan, told me on my arrival that the office could not afford the both of us. Maybe it was the way he said it. I immediately wished him well in his new assignment, and suggested he leave fairly quickly to avoid any embarrassment. He landed on his feet at the Warsaw office of Burson-Marsteller.

I gathered the staff together in the largest room of the Desyatinna office. I simply said follow me, and we will succeed. I said we were going to be just fine, but it would take a lot of hard work. I think I used the old William Faulkner line out of his Nobel Prize acceptance speech: "We will not only prevail, we will endure." It was hokey, but something I said that day bolstered spirits, for all started working like banshees. At the same time, I put a quick end to any extraneous businesses being run out of the office.

In one of his e-mails, Don Cogman said I would need to negotiate the deal with Teresa Dorn, the Burson consultant who had seen fit to choose Mark D'Anastasio over me as Moscow market leader. While I was skeptical, I wasn't suspicious. I merely thought she had made a mistake with Moscow, and this was an entirely different situation.

In fact, had I known then what I know now, I would have thanked her profusely for passing me over for Mark, whose days with the company were numbered. With Burson, I had a limited number of years, no matter how you sliced the bologna. In fact, a few years later, after he left and had returned to Burson, the company saw fit to release my friend Gary Auxier, a fellow who had served as COO in Washington and then led the Philip Morris business. He was 62. The leaders at Burson were becoming younger, it appeared. I really didn't fit into the culture.

The Kyiv office had a long-planned boat ride and picnic on the Dnipro River set for the weekend. Several clients had been invited. However, it wasn't something I would be able to attend. Glen and I were off to Madrid, to arm wrestle Teresa over purchasing the office. We lost one day because we couldn't make connections in time in Zurich, and so arrived on Saturday. The meeting had been moved to Sunday, so we spent the evening drinking cognac and smoking fine Cuban cigars in Plaza Mayor, and plotted what we would say and not say in our meeting.

In the final analysis, it was all rather painless, even for a preliminary round. We had less than an hour-long discussion, and walked away with copies of several agreements that would be discussed with Burson and Young & Rubicam in New York. In the end, we were to pay around $350,000 to take over the recently renovated office and equipment.

In the previous six months, the Kyiv office had lost three major clients. It was my intention to get them all back; and, in fact, over the next couple of years we accomplished this. I divided everyone – absolutely everyone – into four separate and competing new business teams and gave bonuses for business leads. In the final analysis, it wasn't these games that won business, but I do believe they helped us maintain focus. Most of the growth back to profitability came from increasing business from two clients, Philip Morris and Kraft.

We also needed a name, and several were tossed around. At one point, I proposed something with the word "strategic", perhaps it was "Strategic Approaches", the name of our current and long-time newsletter. It was soon discarded for Willard & Payne, since Payne would be the third leg of a partnership we were forming. In the final analysis, I heeded the advice of several close to me and named it The Willard Group. We held that moniker for eight years until we dropped the article and the word "Group" and simply became Willard. To go with a new name, art director Igor Kovriga came up with the duel chaika (seagull) symbol which we still use today.

Then, disaster hit. We organized the business in May, formalized it in July, and a financial crisis hit Eastern Europe in August. We had picked the absolute worst time to launch a business. The crisis, which was to last 20 months, blew through Russia like a hurricane. It gathered steam and made its way into Ukraine. We were to see a 50 per cent loss in the value of Ukrainian currency, the hryvna. Short-term investors scrambled to leave. Everyone was predicting dire consequences, particularly the barroom sages who pretended to know more than anyone else. In reality, no one had a clue, least of all the government. I hastily put together a meeting with the National Bank chairman, Viktor Yushchenko, the man who was later to co-lead the Orange Revolution and end up with the presidency. At the meeting, Yushchenko agreed to host a meeting of nervous multinationals who had invested in Ukraine and were wondering if they were about to lose it all. While the meeting was interesting, it was not all that edifying. People went away scratching their heads over the government's plan or non-plan.

One thing the National Bank did, however, was to freeze money from leaving the country. Because of this, we were unable to repatriate money that Burson-Marsteller had in Ukraine. This actually worked in our favor by giving us a liquidity cushion to weather the storm. At the same time, we protected Burson's money as best as possible from devaluation. As a business during that first year we lost a little money, about $75,000, but we were careful in working with our clients to keep to a minimum both our losses and theirs. As a result, we were to emerge stronger after the crisis. In fact, we didn't retreat during this period, but became inventive in attempting to form new revenue streams. I cannot say that any scheme actually worked, but again, it directed intensity like a red-hot beam to what we needed to do to survive.

As to the crisis itself, I remember discussing various ideas so as not to lose money on the hryvna. For one thing, we paid people in advance, getting money out the door as soon as possible. Scania, the truck manufacturing company, was a client at the time. I remember even considering a plan floated to buy several Scania trucks. Fortunately, that idea was shelved.

Over the years, I have awoken with various ideas. Some were good, others not so. However, when drilling for oil they say that one in 10 is a good percentage. I believe my nocturnally inspired initiatives were somewhat better than that. When I get on to an idea, I rarely let go, and sometimes hold on longer than necessary. I think this is better than not having any ideas at all. For example, the opening of the Moscow office proved fortuitous. After a slow start, it began chugging away, most every month returning a good profit. When that happens, you are considered brilliant. At that time, many were advising that the Moscow market, fresh from its financial crisis, was a bad bet, including the lady who was to become my wife, Tanya. On the other hand, my quick decision to open an office in Istanbul – mainly because it was rather close to Kyiv and I liked the city – left no glory on anyone, especially me.

Mia was born in November 1998, six months after we launched The Willard Group. For Ukraine, Mia is a strange name. It wasn't my first choice, but it was the only one my driver, Vasily, would accept. He rejected Mercedes, which I really liked, because he said it was the name of an automobile. He rejected Porsche for the same reason. Finally, I came to Miata, also a car, but he had never heard of it so agreed. It struck Tanya as a pretty name as well.

In America, one wouldn't normally ask permission from a driver for a child's name, but Vasily had been my driver until I went to Moscow, and was my driver on return, altogether most of a decade. We were friends and many times I visited his house in his village. But, of course, it wasn't with Vasily I had to make the grandest and most difficult of explanations. It was with my wife, and then my daughter, Kelly, and then my son, Rob. Being away from America for a long time tends to promote soap opera episodes, sort of stick-to-the-brain sorghum that can and usually does lead to multi-decibel discussions. It wasn't that way in my case.

On a trip to the U.S. shortly after Mia was born, Becky and I were traveling from our beachfront house in Flagler Beach, Florida to Orlando. At some point in the 45-minute drive, I dropped the bombshell about Mia. As I recall, Becky was driving the maroon Buick Riviera, and maintained a fairly straight path, hardly blinking an eye. At the time, though not officially separated, it was rather obvious we had de facto split, and I suspected that she had a close guy friend at the time. If this were true, I certainly could not complain from the standpoint of crystal clear fairness. We were about to take off on a two-pronged vacation with our children, first to Santa Fe and then back to Disney World. Kelly and her husband would be with us on the first leg, and Rob and his girlfriend were to join us on the second.

However, Kelly and Rob were not to know they had a new sister until a quick trip to Charlotte, North Carolina, where my daughter lived, and Washington, D.C., where my son lived, the following December. Kelly, who thought I was dying of something because I asked to speak to her alone. I told her in the middle of a Charlotte mall, competing with Christmas carols. She was upset, not because of Mia, but because I had not told her sooner. As for Rob, the news had already traveled faster than if issued by CNN, and the three of us, Tanya, Rob and I had a nice dinner at the Monocle on Capitol Hill.

Becky and I were divorced on December 16, 1999, and I married Tanya the next day in a civil ceremony at my sister's home in Palm Bay, Fla. There was a preacher there, but he declined the honor, perhaps feeling he didn't want to put his blessing on something that wouldn't last. The good reverend did play his guitar and sang at the reception. He was a talented songwriter and quite charming. He was also wrong and he was also right: It lasted five more years, which in this world can be a lifetime. Then, it died, slowly, even painfully.

As for the business, we were fortunate in those early days, but very few defining moments hinge totally on the luck of the draw.

We had two sizable clients in Kraft confectionery and with several Philip Morris brands that we helped keep more than competitive. We devoted strong teams to both, worked hard, and came up with creative solutions. Also, the best designers tended to gravitate to Willard, and we were known for our abilities to churn out eye-popping point-of-purchase material, billboards with high impact and commercials that garnered attention far beyond the 30- or 60-second spot.

One of the best initiatives came from then-advertising director David Payne, who selected a largely unknown young songstress, Ani Lorak, to sing the Korona brand song on various commercials. The commercials for the chocolate bar were filmed in exotic locations of Venice, Rio de Janeiro and Buenos Aires. I did not go on these television shoots, leaving it to David who ran the advertising group with Tania Spiridonova, who later became president of advertising.

In my early days of owning an advertising and PR agency in the United States, I loved the excitement of a commercial shoot. However, after concepting, scripting, and directing dozens of commercials, it got to be rather tedious, like watching a snail cross a four-lane highway. My earliest commercials for the former Willard & Arnold agency did well in creative competitions. I found

I was most at home coming up with "issues" spots, those that held a message. For a while, I had several large clients taking the Corporate Social Responsibility road before the phrase was coined, including an anti-smokeless tobacco campaign for Blue Cross and Blue Shield of West Virginia and another spot I particularly liked called "Focus Group." In it, I brought together typical teenagers and spent the day with a facilitator drawing out their fears, dislikes and hopes. It was recorded by a soundman from Memphis, Glen Trew, and Steve Payne, a professional photographer in Charleston, West Virginia, snapped pictures during a nearly all-day session. We spent hours going through pictures and audio tape to come up with the comments and photos that had dramatic impact and edited them into a 60-second spot. The spot won Best of Show in a regional Addy competition.

On coming to Kyiv, I still liked to try my hand in creating good advertising, and virtually all of the company's self-promotion ads were my creation. Most focused on our employees, whom I liked to spotlight. Owning an agency comes with a lot of headaches, but if you are persistent enough you can capture a creative area that is all your own. In my case it was producing company ads. This was exclusively my purview. Would I have liked to go on a commercial shoot to Rio? Of course I would. Would I take someone else's opportunity from them just to tag along? I would not. However, I loved the advertising arena just as much as I did the PR work. People just thought of me more as a PR guy.

On the public relations side of our business, I think the single most important account for us, though it didn't bring in that much money, was organizing then-President Leonid Kuchma's Presidential Press Seminar every three months. That helped us keep a high profile with the press, and solidified our government contacts. We had it for seven years, and continued to organize it sporadically with future governments.

I would like to think that over the next 10 years we specialized in those areas that made us appear more cerebral. We didn't. Given the competitive nature of our business, we played the field, doing everything from the equivalent of brochures and bumper stickers to blowing up the balloons. Along the way, we advised politicians and CEOs how to respond to crises and to the press. We did the heavy lifting, along with the lighter-than-air. That's what you do when you have razor-thin margins, a payroll to meet and you work in risky markets.

During this time, I wrote various books, starting with *Dancing with the Bear: Crisis Management in Eastern Europe*. The book was born of desperation. During the crisis of 1998-99 we didn't know from which direction the next client might come. And even though I had confidence we would weather the storm, I felt a compulsion to place more talents in my portfolio. Being an able crisis manager and letting people know about it was one such. I soon followed this with a book on media training called *"The Accidental Headline"*, hardly more than a 100-page pamphlet. Thus, another union card punched. I had neatly put crisis management and training and media training under my hat. Though the crisis book was self-published at a cost of only $2,000, it ended up bringing in several hundred thousand in new crisis business to the firm.

I had been working on an autobiography over the years. Having walked in the steps of the famous and semi-famous, I felt it was time I jotted down thoughts for my children and grandchildren. However, when it came down to it, I didn't feel I had sufficient material to sustain just an autobiography so I made it more a philosophical book on public relations. It was called *The Flak: A PR Journey*. It was printed in Russian as *PRschik*, meaning the PR guy.

Somewhere along the way, and as I became older, I felt that we in the Yellow Leaf period needed to fight back against society's norm that one was suppose to retire at age 62 or 65, and go tend to the lemon trees. I also realized there was a growing segment out there of people my age that couldn't retire due to accumulated responsibilities, such as multiple families, alimony, child support and the general weight of obligations. Additionally, we Americans were living longer, and really screwing up actuarial charts that were developed decades ago. So, I came forth with an inspirational book for people not aspiring to retire. I called it *"The Portfolio Bubble: Surviving Professionally at 60"*. The book got rave reviews across the board but my distribution network was weak, to say the least.

Another book, written over a period of years, never quite made it to full term, though was released online as *"The Silverback Diaries: The Manager as Hero"*, it was, as much as anything, devoted to my theories on management. However, it was also a book of pet peeves and rants. I found that personal theories can change and rants modified the longer a book is drawn out. I felt it was a good book, but probably not good enough to kill perfectly good trees for the paper it would be printed on. My hope is that one day I will again charge up the hill by writing fiction.

I think I could best describe Willard, the agency, as a good agency with the potential to be better during this time. At times I tend to be loyal to a fault, and held on to certain employees where Burson-Marsteller would have had them out the door long ago. However, in my view, a certain social bond of responsibility does build up if someone has been with a company for several years. Additionally, we had several entangled relationships of sisters, in-laws, etc. – something that goes with the territory when you inherit a business as I did from a government-funded program in Ukraine. This was not, however, an optimal situation, and I had several occasions along the way to put a stop to it, but did not. It wasn't until the most recent worldwide economic crisis that I took those steps, dismissing two long-time employees and relatives of employees who were not great contributors to the company. The problem really wasn't the amount of money expended on them, a relatively small amount. It was about wanting to have the very best people in what I knew would be difficult times. In fact, during this same time I brought in two former employees who had proven their talents and wanted to come back to work at Willard.

In the beginning, we were certainly strongest in advertising, though this was to balance out in the new millennium with several excellent additions to the PR team, including Scott Lewis, a former editor of the Kyiv Post ; Yulia Pushko, as governmental affairs specialist, Elena Babiy, who headed up our publications division but also worked on accounts. Additionally, we had in reserve Galina Aleykina, a smart red-head who rose to the position of executive vice president. She had been with me from the beginning, but had left for a while to become marketing director for a bank.

We already had a very strong Moscow PR team led by Roman Diukarev, and it was starting to take off. He was ably backed up by a dynamo of a young lady, Natasha Shagarina, and the very experienced Andrey Rylski, whose cousin, Maxim, worked in the Kyiv office.

My own contribution came in the form of senior counsel and working primarily at the managing director level both on the public relations and advertising sides. The several columns I wrote for international publications kept our visibility high, along with the books I penned and even the painting exhibitions. The prime minister went out and bought a copy of *PRschik*, the Russian version of the autobiographical book I had written, and I was called to speak at various seminars. During one summer, I did a tour of Ukraine's major universities, giving lectures to hundreds of students.

As an agency, I believe we were more creative than the folks around the corner. Over the years, we had a succession of creative directors, all Ukrainian with the exception of one Russian. I always urged David Payne to step into that role, but he tended to take a backseat to any strong creative we brought on board. Probably the most dominant personality over the years was Roman Stratychuk. Roman looked the part of the typical creative director, complete with earring and long hair. However, he was sufficiently prolific and creative to not just dress the part but to play the part.

While agencies are most often judged by their creativity, I think that should just be one standard. Creativity has nothing to do with a dangling earring, spiked or longish hair, or a Che Guevara t-shirt. Those are affectations manifested by the most conformist of the breed. This is not to say that someone can't be suitably weird, but if everybody is doing it, that which is meant to be unique is commonplace.

I remember a Young & Rubicam creative director from New York who visited our Kyiv office in the dead of a brutal winter. He wore beach flip-flops, no socks. The fellow might have been the Michelangelo of advertising, but to me his elevator was permanently stuck on the mezzanine level.

In 2007, I named a creative director for our public relations group. It was the same person who was managing director for PR in Kyiv. At the time, he was a 53-year-old nearly blind fellow who had previously been editor of the English language Kyiv Post. Scott Lewis didn't look the part. He was short and heavy-set, wore suits a little too snug for his frame, and generally had the look of a kindly and jolly Soviet apparatchik. I picked him because he was the sharpest knife in the drawer when it came to near instantaneous creative ideas. While there were some in the advertising group who felt that a non-Russian or non-Ukrainian speaker could not measure up as a creative person in Ukraine, Scott showed them over time through a series of great ideas. Scott generated the ideas for and the strategies behind some of our best BTL campaigns. However, after about five years, Scott left to sign up with Pulse

Marketing. They offered him the chance to build his own PR shop and more money. I didn't want to lose him and offered to match the Pulse offer. However, at that point he had one foot out the door. In my list of irreversibly bad decisions, I should have paid Scott what he was worth. However, we were in the middle of another recession, and I couldn't see though the fog. Scott's decision to leave meant I had to postpone a carefully planned escape from the day-to-day work of the agency to concentrate on senior counsel, our new magazine, *Willard Marketing Monthly*, and new business. By this time, I had already kicked myself up to chairman and named another CEO. However, it seemed I could not pull myself away from much of the everyday activities. In fact, I was writing most of the new business proposals and also carrying on executive training on media interviews, crisis preparation and how to speak with authority in presentations.

After eight months, I approached Scott again, this time giving him more than a fair offer. He accepted and rejoined the company in September 2010. There was a reason I pursued Scott aggressively. I had made a decision to join forces with All About Brands, based in London, and they had asked me to take on a more global role. I knew I could not do that job without having considerable backup at home. I was overjoyed when Scott had a change of heart.

There is another misconception in our business. Creatives, when it comes to advertising, are not born – as in born with a creative mind. It would be just as odd to have a third eye, as it would to be conceived and delivered without a shred of creativity. All humans are creative in some way. The same creative logic my nine-year-old used a couple of years back to convince me to buy her one more expensive Barbie doll is part and parcel of advertising strategy.

In my view, creativity has to do with intelligence, and not the Einstein variety. If someone is moderately intelligent – can generally tie their shoes after figuring right from left – then they can be creative. Creativity primarily is a learned experience, interestingly applied. The secret to this Holy Grail is hidden not so much behind a mysterious door, but in figuring out what key unlocks the door.

In advertising, we tend to confuse entertainment with creativity. Hence, often the television spots that claim awards at black-tie ceremonies come up short in moving the product or service. A few years back, when the predecessor to The Willard Group was in charge of a USAID program, we produced television spots and print ads that people loved to hate. The ads failed to excite the several focus group cabals put together to test them. However, the ads worked. They made people think. They even made people a little uncomfortable. In short, they moved people to action, which, in this case, meant picking up privatization certificates.

Creativity manifests itself in strange and mysterious ways. The "ring around the collar" spot for Wisk many years back has to be one of the most grating spots ever produced. Yet, it sold sufficient Wisk to fill an ocean. The long and short of it, however, is that creativity is a greatly misunderstood commodity that is often misidentified by a cliquish ad community more intent on – and content to – win awards.

When someone proclaims they are not creative while working at our agency, my first reaction is: Sure you are. If they persist, my second reaction is: Then why are you working in an ad agency? The same is true for public relations.

Chapter
12

Spreading Our Wings

Being a businessman was not something to which I aspired. When I was young, I wanted to be a flying missionary (as in my own plane) to the heathens in Africa. Though I eventually got the plane, a twin-engine Beechcraft Baron used in my business, I became rather agnostic as time went by. As I grew into my teens, I took the famous Kuder test to determine my career interests. The fellow who gave the test said I cheated.

Of course, those weren't his exact words. He said I over emphasized wanting to be a social worker to the extreme, thereby making the test not valid, or not as valid. This, however, I believe was a junior year phase. Organized social work was soon placed in another orbit, though I have always pushed clients to what some call Corporate Social Responsibility but I simply call good business.

One day, when my father was stationed at Upper Heyford Air Force Base in England, I went to the base cinema and saw a flick based on an Ernest Hemmingway novel. I suddenly wanted to be a foreign or war correspondent, and that held with me like sap on a tree for years. In reality, my only stint as a foreign correspondent came early, covering those NATO exercises in Turkey when I was just 22, working for the *Tampa Times*. It lasted less than a month and nary a shot was fired in anger. However, I did become a journalist, though we old timers in the profession prefer to be called reporters, or even newspapermen or women. Most of my early reporter career was spent with that grand old wire service of days gone by, United Press International.

My yearning to write for the public in some form led to the creation of something that was to be very expensive and never make any money, but gave me and others huge enjoyment. In 1999, we launched *The Ukrainian Observer*, first as an online publication, then as a quarterly that soon became a monthly. Common sense rarely catches the same train as that of hubris, and we are left standing on the platform shoeless and without socks. That's an exaggeration, of course, for eventually, if we search hard enough, we find a business rationale for untamed lunacy.

For years I have told the story about why I started the magazine. It had to do with finding out how much it was going to cost to place a company ad in the weekly *Kyiv Post*. "We could start our own publication for that amount," I blustered. We couldn't, but we did.

We doggedly published the magazine for seven years and a succession of editors. During its most controversial period, my brother Glen was the editor, and though a few toes were stepped on, I think the magazine was best during this period. This is not to take away from other editors, Scott Lewis for a brief period (He was too good to languish on something that didn't pay the freight), John Marone, who was transferred for a while to another part of our business, or Jim Davis, a 70-something long-time expat who had more energy in his seventh decade than people half his age.

In the very early days, I also served as editor, but used the moniker Harvey Strange, and an editor's picture in the magazine of the Hathaway Shirt guy of ad fame, the one with an eye patch. I simply didn't want people thinking it was a one-man band, which it wasn't.

Under Glen, the publication took the U.S. Embassy head-on when bureaucrats wouldn't allow a ship captained by a

Ukrainian patriot to dock and visit United States ports. Glen felt the friendship tour by this private individual was good for Ukraine and good for the United States. He couldn't see the logic in the Captain's crew not being able to leave the ship when it docked in America. He believed they deserved visas. He didn't shy away from other arguments, as well, often taking a divergent view from the publisher. I, however, liked having a magazine with varied opinions, and we would often have dueling articles on such issues as capital punishment with Glen taking the conservative pro side and me taking the right side.

Few people in the business community knew my role in the Observer, even though my name was on the masthead as publisher. They did know that I contributed one, maybe two columns a month to the publication. But I also did the concept for the cartoon cover as well as the four cartoons that became trademarks of the magazine. I also managed to develop company ads and a company newsletter that were inserted into the rather eclectic magazine. It was probably Kyiv's best-read yet under-supported publication.

Each month, the magazine grew in expense. At first, we just had a couple of color pages, but eventually ran full-color throughout the magazine. We paid people to write stories, and printing costs continued to rise. For a while we had an ad salesman, the genuine article, a fellow who could sell sand in the Sahara. However, this super salesman, an Irishman named Gerald Harty, couldn't bring in sufficient revenue for it to pay for itself. But we had fun.

The magazine gave birth to another informal organization, The Saturday Club, in which four to five people most responsible for the magazine sat around each weekend at a pub called O'Brien's, stuffed ourselves with the big Homemade Breakfast, and decided editorial issues. The group included Glen, Lewis, Davis, Robert Reed and me. The average age of the group was about 60.

In the summer of 2006, I wrote a column about The Ukrainian Observer that described the give-and-take of The Saturday Club:

The Saturday Club

"By all accounts, the last issue of The Ukrainian Observer was to be titled 'The Case Against NATO'. It wasn't. Jim Davis, the editor, perhaps being more circumspect than me, the publisher, came out with the pros and cons of Ukraine and NATO.

"There is a case, though a flimsy one, to be made for Ukraine's entry into NATO. In geopolitical terms, I view it as unmitigated disaster. Jim has about eight years on me – we are both well into our yellow leaf stage – so is probably wiser, certainly more diplomatic.

"These are the types of things we discuss at our editorial meetings each weekend at O'Brien's Pub, what we call The Saturday Club. We gobble up artery clogging breakfasts that would, should and will kill mere mortals. Jim has opted for the 'lighter fare', a rack of bacon, three fried eggs and butter-drenched toast. He fools no one, least of all his cardiac specialist.

"Other charter members are Scott Lewis, a former editor who now heads up PR at Willard in Kyiv, and my brother, Glen, also a former editor, but now in self-imposed exile in Western Ukraine.

All this is to suggest that the ingredients in The Ukrainian Observer, as in O'Brien's breakfasts, happen not so much by happenstance but through rather helter-skelter planning. Still, when the June issue came out, I was surprised to see an overkill of 12 pages devoted to NATO, even though I had glanced over it just prior to printing.

"You see, I have work other than the UO. I am the titular head of an advertising and public relations agency that has spread to three countries and employs about 100 people. I travel a good bit, and am involved to some degree in all of our client activities.

"My contribution to the magazine is this Random Notes column,

which I have been writing for nearly eight years, and the Workplace column, which is in its second year. I also concept the rather obscure cartoons, and have for these many years.

"My view on the magazine will soon be Jim's view. I want a rather iconoclastic, somewhat eclectic rag that takes a stand. I don't want it to be another chamber of commerce-type publication. I want it to have 'sustained rage.'

"While sustained rage is a phrase coined by my late friend, Charleston (West Virginia) Gazette publisher Ned Chilton, I believe my brother, Glen, probably comes closest to my view in this regard. He the archconservative and I the soggy liberal seem to agree that a magazine that shrinks from controversy is a collection of just so many dead trees pressed together.

"I admire magazines like The Economist which come out with front-page headlines: 'Berlusconi Must Go', whether I agreed with the proposition or not. Often I don't agree with this particular magazine, but I read it faithfully every week. This is what I yearn for with The Ukrainian Observer.

There is, of course, genetic conflict in owning a public relations and advertising agency and in publishing a magazine that takes on issues. There is a very good possibility that the folks who pay us money and keep us in business will disagree with those views.

Hence, when The Observer cartoon gently chides Amcham (the American Chamber of Commerce in Ukraine) for its elitist "Captains of Industry" – a term that conjures up the Vanderbilts, the Lord Beaverbrooks and the Rockefellers – and is truly silly and Babbit-like, certain clients and would-be clients wince.

"Many have the feeling that it is the work of Robert Reed, our external affairs vice president and go-to guy, as in go to Amcham, go to EBA, go to the Danish Ambassador's reception. The Observer character bears a more than passing resemblance to Robert, as it should.

"Over the years, The Ukrainian Observer has not hesitated to take on established institutions. One was the U.S. Embassy, which cries out "to give me your huddled masses" but then, in times past, has left them shivering in the cold and made them pay for visa applications when they had little chance of being chosen for the promised land.

"On the other hand, the UO has praised the embassies, particularly the British Embassy and on occasion the U.S. Embassy, when they have acted in truly admirable ways. The British Embassy received one of our First Class Service Awards, as I recall.

"In any event, The Ukrainian Observer is evolving. It is now in full color, and if the ad guy sells enough ads it will continue to be. It makes it onto various airlines, including Ukraine International, Aerosvit and the outside trolley of British Airways. It can be found at major watering holes, hotels and restaurants.

"The Observer is also chock full of legitimate ads. By this I mean ads that were actually purchased, no barter agreements, no kickbacks to marketing directors. In nearly seven years, it has matured as a magazine and an institution in its own right.

"Much of this evolution has to do with suggestions from our readers. Much has come from the Saturday Club gatherings, which on occasion have led to within a hair's width of knockdown, drag-out arguments. This is what has made it fun.

"In fact, join us some Saturday, 11 a.m. at O'Brien's. We'll pull up another chair or two.

"Breakfast will be on Editor Davis."

Early into The Ukrainian Observer I began using Reed, who looked vaguely like a thin Ernest Hemmingway, as a model for a cartoon called The Observer. From time to time, he carried a knapsack, and so I included this element into the cartoon, and, for good measure, added a small portable scooter which he always had at his side or on his back, a fictional affectation.

Robert was Mr. Outside. A member of the European Business Association's board of directors (though he was not European), Robert attended virtually every possible civic and club function for the company, from American Chamber of Commerce events to embassy social functions. The "Observer" impression took hold, and over time, Robert became one of the most easily recognized expatriates in Kyiv.

Every expat came to Willard for different reasons. Reed was stranded in Kyiv when a project he was working on having to do with providing prosthetics to people who couldn't afford them went sour. This was the first few months of the company, but we took him on at a rather low salary during the economic crisis. A former special forces medic in the U.S. Army, Reed turned into a valuable asset for his willingness to do just about anything to stay in Ukraine where he had fallen in love with a pediatrics doctor named Larisa.

If Robert was Mr. Outside, I was Mr. Inside. In some respects, I am just the opposite of the person one conjures when contemplating the typical public relations person. I am not outgoing. Standing around at a cocktail party balancing a drink and a plate is torture for me. While I can crank up a crowd with a speech, I have always been rather shy unless the center of attention, and then I have this out-of-body experience and perform. In 15 years, I have managed only one American Chamber event in Kyiv, though my Moscow manager, Roman Diukarev, did manage to drag me to a chamber breakfast in Moscow once.

I write the above as if I am proud of it. I am not. It is just me, a solitary fellow who would rather write, paint, develop a strategic proposal or take a walk than commit time at events to which I find dreadful. I like the people at those events, but as individuals, not in a group setting. If asked, and I have been on occasion, I can speak before these types of groups, but I would not be one of the people listening to me. On the other hand, I love quality contact with people in and out of the business community on a one-on-one basis and try to have a battery of lunches through the work week.

I feel that my best relationships have developed over private lunches with a managing director or marketing or PR director sitting across from me. I enjoy making business acquaintances, but not in a gang-bang atmosphere. It seemed somewhat hypocritical to invite many of these same expat civic leaders to the several painting exhibitions I have held, but I did, and was grateful they came and a few even bought paintings.

I am not sure from where this social timidity stems, though on one level I believe it was the result of having to go to too many receptions and too many campaign events as a political reporter and later working in politics. For a while, many people thought my brother Glen was Mike, for he was much more visible, though generally he also stayed away from the organized meetings as well.

However, being a CEO of a company takes all types. My view was that I could be a better manager if I stayed slightly above the fray and Robert did those things that he thoroughly enjoyed and I avoided them. Both avenues seemed to work in pulling in new business. We were, especially in the first eight years, very successful. We were to have some rough times, but that's what make doing business in risky markets interesting.

Over the years, we did our best to have fun as an agency. We mostly succeeded, or else we would not have kept a core group of thoroughly competent people for so many years. For most of Willard's existence, we had an annual party to which a few clients were invited. One such event was especially memorable, and was mostly organized by my executive assistant and a senior vice president in our organization, Oksana Yerofeyeva. Oksana has been with me from the latter days of the education program. She's my Radar O'Reilly, seeming to know what I want before I knew what I wanted. She has also been a confidante and friend.

I wanted to shake up things just a little; a germ of an idea was supplied by our PR director in Kyiv, Scott, who mentioned something about a fake oligarch showing up at the party. This was a good month before the event. However, I liked the idea and carried it nearly to extremes.

I hired a clown who actually looked like a Ukrainian oligarch and had him come into the office the day before the party and call me out of an important meeting with senior staff.

He poked his head in the door of the conference room, and was flanked by two "bodyguards". I dutifully and nervously told those present that I needed to leave the room, and then accompanied the oligarch around the office as he pretended to make an inspection. When I got back to the meeting, all asked me who the fellow was. Just an acquaintance, I answered, pretending nervousness.

The next night, however, the oligarch showed up at the party, and I had instructed several photographers to cluster around him shooting pictures as if he were someone rather important. Then, as I was about to start the night's festivities, I identified him as an Eastern Ukrainian businessman and my new partner. We kept up the charade for a good half hour until I saw that my real partner, David Payne, was so angry he was about to explode. While the music played and dinner was being served I went over to David to explain to him that the oligarch was a clown.

"I know he's a clown," David seethed, which meant he had no idea and was just adopting my characterization.

"Really David. I promise. He's really a clown."

David eventually calmed down, and we went back to different parts of the ceremonies. Most in the audience remained fooled and shocked until the oligarch appeared again, this time with his troupe and in a clown outfit.

I had always said to my staff that I want a company that had fun and made a profit. If we make a profit, and I don't have fun, I didn't want to work for the company. If we didn't make a profit, and had fun, I couldn't work for the company.

Of a more serious nature, we lived by a mantra I put on the top stairs of our second office: "Every agency says it is creative, gets results and is strategic. If every agency is saying that, this must just be average. We must do better."

I think most of time we achieved this, though a few times we did come up short and I hated it.

Chapter
13

A Way of Doing Business

The books that Harvard Business School professors write probably would place doing business closer to a science than an art. But I never went to Harvard and what I learned was primarily on-the-job training.

Until I opened my first business in West Virginia on the cusp of my fourth decade, I had never seen a balance sheet. I had one accounting course in college and passed only by promising the professor I would never take another. But, I like keeping score, and I find that is what business is all about. Take more money in then you spend and you put a point on the board each month. Pretty basic stuff.

The art part comes in managing and motivating people, particularly in the kinds of businesses with which I have been involved. We don't make anything. At the end of the work day, we haven't boxed up a single widget. We have no product inventory on the shelf. We deal primarily in ideas, new ideas since we have to reinvent to stay ahead of the competition.

Though it is a trite expression, our inventory – our people – do go home at the end of the day. Or do they? At my company, I have tried to change that by coming up with the 24-hour workday. This doesn't mean I am a slave master, just the opposite. This is where we get into the hazy and lofty air of business being more art than anything else.

This is where Galaxy Thinking takes us, from the sublime to the ridiculous and back to what I call the Holy Cow Common Sense Factor. Where a direction which could be thought of as rather revolutionary, even odd and bizarre, becomes normal, because it is the only way to do business in even a small non-retail professional company in the 21st century.

Sit back for a few moments while I treat you to a Willard-ism, a view I expressed in "The Silverback Diaries" and a way of thinking and working I have instilled in my own company. This didn't come about overnight, but in phases. We are still trying to perfect it.

The 24-hour Workday

We live and work today in 24-hour time segments, and it really makes no difference if you are behind a desk, driving your car, taking a shower or washing the dishes.

Time is not a thing, but a state of mind. Intellectual work – that creative and strategic thought you bring to your job – cannot be lassoed and contained within a glass cubicle any more than it can be sustained in a Petri dish for study. No self-respecting professional looks at the clock on his desk and automatically shuts his or her brain down when the sun goes down. It is, in fact, a misnomer to label work by that traditional name, sort of like calling a car a horseless carriage or a fancy refrigerator an icebox. My suggestion would be to simply call it paid time.

Paid time can and does occur anywhere, and it is a 24-hour phenomenon. To my knowledge, there is nothing written down, biblical or otherwise, that prescribes a workday as consecutive hours, usually eight and usually during the day. We as professionals have become too sophisticated, too mobile, and too global to think in the narrow confines of traditional paid time. Business time is all the time and it has been for at least the last decade or so. Many companies have yet to realize this. Once they do, they will also realize that the paid time of the individual worker can be adjusted to fit global circumstances, and not just the mere convenience of fellow workers, even bosses. For those who prefer the 9-to-5 or -6 tradition, fine, but all should realize that it is simply another option, and probably not the best one.

The 24-hour paradigm recognizes that one professional taking a long lunch to shop for disposable nappies is not mutinous but, most likely, necessary. Life is complicated, more so, I believe, for female colleagues where tradition has bestowed on them many more "real life" responsibilities, like grocery shopping and making sure the kids are ready for school. There has been some societal change in this, but it is far from a sea change, particularly in more conservative and non-secular countries.

It all goes back to simply this: Getting the job done, and done well. This should be thought of as a 24-hour assignment, and not the rigidity of the eight-hour workday or the 40-hour week. Not to pick on the French, but by dumbing down an already irrelevant 40-hour work week to an even less relevant 35 hours for professionals is not only to surrender Waterloo but also toss in a couple of cases of Perrier Jouet Vintage Grand Brut to boot. As I write this, there are some signs that the French government has also come to its senses.

What about weekends? The word 'weekend' has been around for less than 100 years. Weekends are not sacrosanct, unless the employee wishes them to be. Most professional work is performed in sustained time segments, not in a forced all-day march. Think about what you did today, and most likely you can identify specific efforts put forth, combined with work/personal time (Did you check your stocks on the boss's so-called dime?), a measure of work/relax time (Did you have a couple of tea breaks?), and work/necessary time (Did you have an errand to run that was unrelated to the business?) If you think in terms of sustained time segments, they can and should occur at any time, even on a Saturday, a Sunday or even holidays.

Most of the work we do as professionals occurs within the boundaries of our own mind. I don't know about you, but I have never found the switch to completely turn off work during a weekend. Likewise, my mind wanders – as does yours – during traditional work time. It is in the nature of human beings.

Also, if you like your work, it is not work. If you think creatively about your work outside of what some would consider normal work hours, then it is not an invasion of your private time. It is merely work-related recreation.

If you don't like your work, you should change jobs. It is as simple as that. There is absolutely no reason for a work/serf society in the 21st century. I know what you are thinking: This old fool is speaking of an idyllic situation, one without the worries of everyday life, such as paying bills, college tuition and the myriad of other responsibilities that hang around us like Spanish moss.

I look at it this way: I once had an old Porsche Targa that could go zero to 60 miles per hour in nothing flat. That's sort of like life. It's over in no time at all. George Elliott said it best: "It is never too late to be who you might have been." Quoting somebody more contemporary, Steve Jobs, chief of Apple: "Your time is limited, so don't waste it living someone else's life." Jobs, by the way, knows of which he speaks. He is a cancer survivor.

Can everyone survive in this new liberal (I use the word loosely here) world? Of course not, but those folks were also the slackers of the old world. They were then and are now like pilot fish attached to a shark, carried on by the momentum of another. By definition, the term "professional" carries with it minimal obligations, the first being to insure that the company makes a profit. If certain pilot fish don't contribute greatly to this effort, as my restaurateur friend Erwin Asam, proprietor of the Bavarian Inn and Lodge in Shepherdstown, West Virginia, would say on occasion – avoiding the word "fired" – "You quit."

The concept of the 24-hour workday is not that new and something I arrived at over a period of time. It was not an epiphany; and, I confess, the jury is still out. It takes an extraordinary amount of professionalism and sense of work responsibility to live within the blue-sky framework of unlimited freedom. That which does not have walls, does have fences of papier-mâché. Self-rule at work is a philosophy based in the writings of John Locke and Jean Jacques Rousseau. I believe if Benjamin Franklin were around today – in the age of the Internet – he would have proposed it, reveled in it, for he was never a 9-to-5 guy, preferring to sleep very late each morning. Information today travels at light speed, while in the days of Franklin, given a strong tail wind, it was a 40-day jaunt from England to the New World by ship.

My former partner, David, never got the hang of the 24-hour workday, and complained when staff didn't follow his more traditional 9-to-6 regimen. In this regard, we were at loggerheads. We actually had different views on most aspects of work. It is a wonder the partnership lasted 10 years. That it did was probably a tribute to David more so than to me. Over the years, I tossed a number of curves at him, and most of the time he took it in stride. However, a few times we hurled insults as if they were bean balls tossed at high velocity. I regret that now.

While diverging slightly from my "a way of working" scheme – it is related of course – to relationships. My belief is that leadership must be earned, not bestowed. It is rarely an entitlement, even if you own the business and your name is clearly written on the door. This is particularly true of the personal services business, where the leader is the team captain but whose livelihood depends on each professional employee carrying out his or her assignment. Additionally, the employee has been entrusted with clients, and often loyalty builds between the client and the employee, with the company being an orbiting and perhaps not necessary third party.

This is dangerous, and it is why I do my best to develop an on-going relationship with the person at the top of the food chain, generally the managing director, but occasionally it is a powerful marketing or public relations director.

It has been said by some managers that it is best to churn employees, that those that stay around too long become too complacent, set in their ways, and are not willing to accept new assignments. True. But I believe these barriers to company growth must be overcome. The leadership of our company has been with me for the better part of 16 years, this includes our president of advertising and the executive vice president handling our largest account. It includes our media director, our IT director and our webmaster. It includes our deputy finance director. In fact, the nine people in leadership positions (executive or senior vice presidents) in our Kyiv office have a total 115 years service to Willard, or an average of 11 years each. That's a long time.

However, they are each in their positions because they earned them. I believe strongly in reciprocal loyalty. That is, if an employee is willing to stick it out with me through thick and thin, through financial crises and personal upheavals, then I will walk over hot coals for him or her. I don't like to talk about businesses becoming like a family, because my only kids are five in number and they are, indeed, my children. However, we have come pretty damn close to it.

One of my primary tools for communication is a short memo I write each day entitled Willard Notes. This takes time, generally, about 20-minutes each evening. I offer up a quote of the day, often something I have made up, but which in some way relates to current activity, and then I list my schedule of appointments.

What follows is a litany of items that can meander off in several directions, depending on mood and moment. I use it to praise individually, but occasionally scold as a group. It reeks with Willard-isms that sometimes go beyond the translator's abilities for the few in our office who do not speak English. Sometimes it is opinionated and untamed, a rather interesting read. At other times, it is as flat as road kill. I am told that our staff knows generally what to expect from me the rest of the day by just reading Willard Notes. I hate that.

Usually, the notes discuss what happened the previous day in each of the offices and what is planned for that day and perhaps several days into the future. Willard Notes has served as a daily diary and a history of sorts, for much of what I write here has been refreshed in my mind by simply reviewing this simple communication I devised more than 25 years ago when I opened my first company in West Virginia.

A Belief in Service

When I was 12, I sold donuts door to door for the Thompson Company. My territory was a subdivision next to my own in Orlando, Florida's Azalea Park area. I rarely came home without the 12 dozen and six half dozen packages being sold. I received a dollar, three days a week, and thought I was rich. When I turned 16 I bagged groceries for the Piggly Wiggly in Cordele, Georgia. After a couple of painful lessons where I put cans on top of Mrs. Brown's peaches, I was the best bagger they had. By the end of each day, my pants were weighted down with tips. There was one reason for this: Service. I did more than put groceries in a bag. I create a dialogue with the client by the time I had reached his or her car in the parking lot. While still a servant relationship, it was a friendly and respectful one.

I figure a client can forget and forgive an occasional mistake, maybe even a lapse in judgment if it is not too costly, but only if you give extraordinary service. This is my mantra. I want our people to treat the whole client, not just the immediate problem, event or campaign. I want them to be there for the client 24 hours a day, and not just pay lip service to the very trite saying of 24/7 availability.

That's just one of the reasons why we have the 24-hour workday.

This is why at the turn of the century, I instituted what I called First Class Service and even hired a director for the program.

She was pert and pretty, but most of all she was good. She was a waitress, and I was a customer at a Black Sea resort in Nessebar, Bulgaria. It was the summer of 2001, a time when I wore a black eye-patch like Calico Jack, the pirate.

In a few months, I was to have surgery on the bum eye. The menacing patch was not an affectation, but necessary medical equipment. Otherwise, the so-called "good" eye saw spots and shimmers, sort of what I would imagine a 1960s LSD trip would have been like if I had tried the stuff – which, of course, I did not.

My then-wife and I had our first of several vacation dinners at the seaside establishment, and through the luck of the draw, Julia was our waitress. Her English was fair, and she went out of her way to explain the menu that was in Bulgarian. She didn't hover over us like a plane in a holding pattern, but she did seem to be there every time we wanted to move the dinner onward. She was also good with our daughter Masha who was with us, chatting her up as if the two were about the same age. They were not.

The next night we went back to the same restaurant, not because the food was extraordinary, for it was the same fare found in numerous eateries along the coast; greasy pork, scraggly chicken and beef too tough to chew. We went back for the service. I was curious as to what makes the Julia-types tick, and whether they come with a "nice" gene built in, or is it an acquired trait. She was scurrying around like a water bug at the edge of a pond, hardly causing a wake. Amazing, I thought.

The second time we were not so lucky. A young gentleman was our waiter. He was adequate, but clearly did not measure up to the previous night's attention. However, before long, we saw that Julia had started to direct our dinner service, even though we were not at her table. The service picked up measurably, so much so that the third night of our vacation – next to our last – was spent at the same restaurant. This time, Julia again waited on our table.

"How would you like a job in our company in Kyiv?" I asked, out of the blue. "We could use a great receptionist." At that time, I didn't know whether she even typed. I didn't care. A computer can be taught in a couple of weeks. Some people, no matter how long they are at the job, never get the concept of service. They are tone deaf when it comes to the concept, even though they might be able to do calculus and play a piano like Sergei Rachmaninoff.

Here I was, the old and odd fellow in the black eye-patch, the adornment that conjured up images of white slavery and bottles of too much rum, asking the 22-year-old Julia if she would like to, in essence, run away and take a job as a receptionist in my company; and yes, in a far away and strange land. It was not that far-fetched, for she had a Russian mother and did speak perfect Russian, as well as Bulgarian, and, as noted, her English was passable.

She said she would like to join us – actually she gushed because I was offering her more money in a month than she would make all summer waiting tables in Bulgaria. But first, she would have to ask her mother. This is a corner of the world where women are bought and sold, where unscrupulous thugs kidnap young girls, take their passports and keep them as chattel. She didn't know me, even though I did come with a fairly respectable looking family in tow, and had ordered the right wine at dinner, something red, I believe.

There was too much at stake. By this time, I was determined to hire Julia. I asked her if I could go with her to see her mother. I had this image of Julia attempting to describe to her mother this lecherous old man she met while she waited on tables. He wore a black-eye patch and spoke with the hoarse whisper of a Jack Palance. He was truly evil.

In the end, she was brought on, and worked first as our receptionist for three years, and then headed up the first months of what became known as The Willard Group's First Class Service program. Hiring Julia was a no-brainer. She had service written all over her. She wore it like she wore her faint perfume, ever present, not overwhelming, but just so right. When she left, I shed a crocodile tear, and went looking for someone with Julia's unique talents. I searched most of the globe, but in the end that person, Irina, was right down the street, a waitress at O'Brien's Pub.

That Pirate Thing

"Now and then we had hopes that if we lived and were good, God would permit us to be pirates." – Mark Twain.

For more than a year, we were pirates, swashbuckling, one-eyed rogues of commerce and Khreschatyk Street. It occurred because we were once again in crisis, another career-defining moment that will be described later. However, I felt our company needed more than a jolt, it needed a personality change. We had operated for years in a cocoon of security, wrapped in the wonders of regular cash from the likes of Philip Morris, Colgate and Kraft. Events were to transpire that seriously threatened this calm, a tornado blew in from the West and we were directly in its path. So, from this day forward, I said in December 2005, we are pirates. Pirates, by God. But good pirates.

I find that managers must be predictable in matters of fairness but unpredictable when it comes to waging commercial battle. That is why in the economic crisis of 1998, our agency charged instead of retreated and did the same in the recession of 2009, the philosophy being that the best time to score is when the other team is sitting on the bench.

In 2005 the threat came in from larger agencies with whom we were affiliated and to whom we had been loyal. They wanted a wholly owned office in Kyiv and, in essence, wanted to shut us down – put us out of business. So, I named all aboard the good ship Willard pirates. We would henceforth act and be like pirates. If there were to be no loyalty to us after all these years, then we would battle them toe-to-toe. And that we did. Since this book is, for the most part, a chronological account, I will stick to the affectations and not the nuts and bolts that come later.

However, I awoke one morning with an oppressive feeling that the only way we could go into battle against our antagonists – Young & Rubicam and its parent holding company, WPP – was to morph, to shape-shift into a more aggressive character. At the time, we had matured as an agency, both in age and in habits. We had grown accustomed to being on autopilot for too long, and the only threats we had were from an occasional client problem that generally was solved by the end of the day, or at least by the end of the week. The people I had known at 25 were now approaching 40. I had seen their kids grow, had seen them through marriages, illnesses and divorces.

There was some resistance to the pirate thing. Perhaps some thought it childish when the skull and crossbones flags were put up around the agency, and Willard Notes carried a pirate flag. Some perhaps thought it corny when I handed gold-plated imitation Spanish doubloons for great client work. I didn't care. I wanted to focus attention on a threat that could take food off our tables, and threatened our very existence as an agency. Ironically, it was the Moscow office that really got into the spirit of things, and went out of their way to have pirate t-shirts printed.

To say that a gimmick is an unqualified success is often a contradiction in terms. It is by its very nature an act, a facade. Perhaps it won't help but it can't hurt. I felt I needed something to jumpstart the agency. We needed to go from peacetime complacency to war footing in a fairly short time. I wanted our people to wake up in the morning wanting to beat the dog-ass opposition, and at that time, I saw that opposition as our former advertising partner agency.

Over the years, there were many digressions and transgressions into management absurdities. There once was the time I gave everyone a $50 bonus with only one string attached: Each person had to spend it on someone else in the office, and, in doing so, it had to in some way benefit that person's continuing life education. Several bought books, but one inventive person purchased for another a full-body massage, feeling that this tension reducer would contribute most to one's well being and education. I approved it.

When it comes right down to it, though, what I have done in Ukraine isn't much different than what I did in my first tenure as head of an ad and PR agency. One afternoon I closed the office and took everyone – at that time 25 employees – to see the new Batman movie that was playing down the street.

I have a philosophy of running a business. It is not goofy, though some might describe it as weird. I codified it in our Personnel Manual, which is the shortest such document in the history of business. Self-proclaimed music outlaw David Allan Coe wrote a song about pickups, and moms, and trains and prison and drunks and called it the perfect country and western song:

Well, I was drunk the day my Mom got out of prison,
And I went to pick her up in the rain,
 But before I could get to the station in my pickup truck,
She got run over by a damned old train.

Well, I sincerely believe I have written the all-time perfect employee manual. This one, of course, is written for a public relations and advertising agency. Yours might be a sentence or two shorter or longer. Take a look and see if you don't agree with me.

The Willard Group Employee Manual

Preamble: Every agency says it is creative, strategic and gets results. If everyone is doing it, then this is just being average. We must be better.

Section 1: Imagination

Use your imagination. We are in the imagination business and the idea business. Our people – all our people – are imagination engineers.

Section 2: Judgment

Do your best, and use your best judgment. If we all do this, The Willard Group will succeed beyond our dreams.

Section 3: Difference

We will be strategically different. Calculated risk is part of the fun and interest of being in business. Be a little weird sometimes.

Section 4: Our business

We are not in the advertising business. We are not in the PR business. We are in the client problem-solving business, and often that takes great advertising and PR solutions, or some variation thereof.

Section 5: Human Resources and Benefits

We will be imaginatively ad hoc as it relates to holidays, salary and other benefits. We will endeavor to surpass all other agencies in our pursuit of a better life for our best employees. The others need to strive to be best. Effort counts. Success counts more.

Section 6: Change

Don't be afraid of it. Hold on to your hat, and enjoy the ride. Better yet, be an agent for change.

Section 7: Mistakes

Make a few. If you don't, you're not using that imagination. Don't make the same mistake twice.

Section 8: Dress

We don't believe in casual Fridays. We have no dress code.

You have joined a professional organization. So, it would stand to reason you would want to dress professionally, especially if you come into contact with clients who are dressed for the business day. You never know when a client will be in the office.

I refer you to the section on judgment.

Exceptions: Creative Directors and other creatives can have spiked hair and nose rings and wear t-shirts that say Long Live Ho Chi Minh. Don't try to use them as an excuse to dress unprofessionally. This is the nature of the business. Yes, we have a double standard.

Chapter
14

Time Is a Not A Renewable Resource and Other Sorrows

Some things mellow with age, but I feel that if my motor were to be at idle for any length of time I would stagnate, and be like some green goop at the edge of a dead or dying pond. I enjoy my highs and am tolerant of my lows whenever they come howling into my consciousness. I do try to make allowances for this, though at times I have not been particularly successful.

While this book is chronological and it was my intent to be a character actor and not the star, I nonetheless thought it would be helpful, even interesting, to drag in a few of my outtakes when it comes to the art of doing business.

They are in no particular order, and while they might be instructive to people in the advertising and public relations business, they are by no means exclusive to those niche segments. They are universal truths as seen through my eyes only, or maybe just "grain of truth" assertions about which your mama always warned you.

Popcorn, not Time, is a Renewable Resource

You probably thought the most important thing in your life were those 33 RPM Doris Day records, that bruised baseball signed by Sandy Koufax and, perhaps, your three kids.

The kids are fairly important, assuming they are housebroken, but by far the most important thing in your life is your time. Let's face it; we only have so many ticks in life and then we are out of here. We become great topsoil, or maybe sit on the mantel in a somber urn until the cat accidentally knocks us over. Then, we are damned difficult to extract from the Persian carpet.

Time is not a renewable resource, and it never will be. Popcorn is a renewable resource. If time were renewable, Einstein would have discovered the theory back in the 1930s and we would be, in fact, immortal – at least in theory.

The other day a client called our Moscow office at the exact time he was supposed to arrive. He said he was caught in traffic and would be an hour and a half late. Caught in traffic? Where? London? Tokyo? Admittedly, the traffic in Moscow can be like a colony of freeze-dried ants. However, everyone knows this, and the rule is to leave a little earlier.

The client is not always right. These folks put three people on hold for an hour and a half. They are thieves. They did not take our money; they took our time, which in our business, as the cliché goes, is the same as money. If the transgression had been committed by anyone other than a client, I would have shouted, "Imbeciles." I use the terms imbecile and cretin with regularity and impunity. They are polite and G-rated substitutes for words most often used in gangster movies written and directed by Quentin Tarantino.

Today being inconsiderate of others is a serious and fatal ailment leading to the death of time. It is particularly prevalent in the business world. Most of us value our own time, but we are less considerate of the time of colleagues. It is as if those golden Rolexes are meant only for decoration and, if you are the low-life sort, getting laid by the simple-minded subordinate with a thigh tattoo. They obviously have nothing to do with measuring time and people arriving for meetings at an appointed and agreed-upon hour.

The Goddamit Man

I call the late Geoff Nightingale the "Goddamit man". No, that's not entirely correct; I call him the "GODDAMIT MAN." Geoff had many assignments over the years for Burson-Marsteller, but the one and only time I met him he was refereeing one of those silly group-gropes in New York aimed at coming up with a mission statement for the company. It was more a practice exercise in team building than useful assignment. In fact, I thought at the time, it was a total waste of time, though it was good to see colleagues that – lacking such get-togethers – rarely had the opportunity to exchange ideas.

The meeting was due to start at 9 a.m., which is relatively normal for these sorts of activities, and people began filing in a few minutes earlier, taking advantage of the coffee, pastries and juice at the table in the back of the room. Moreover, there were the usual small groups of chatter and polite conversation, some of us not having seen one another since the previous similarly boring exercise.

The clock hit 9:10 and I casually glanced at Geoff at the front of the room. He was serenely sitting on a stool, gazing out at the gathering crowd. Then it became 9:15, and Nightingale truly had the continence of a nightingale, that oh so small songbird belonging to the thrush family. The gathering continued with catch-up palaver, snatches of conversation really going nowhere. Frankly, no one was really anxious to begin the session, and Nightingale was a bearded stranger to most of us.

Then, it became 9:20, and absolutely no one was paying attention to Nightingale who apparently in the last five minutes had moved off his perch, and was standing in the center of the room.

"GODDAMIT. GODDAMIT," he shouted.

We all of course took notice, or what notice one can take when one is in shock. Generally, the demeanor of these meetings leans toward a congeniality that would put Sinclair Lewis' famous Mr. Babbitt to shame. This coarse and loud interruption caused coffee cups to rattle on tiny saucers.

"Goddamit," he repeated, a little softer this time. "How dare you waste my time? You have taken 20 minutes from my life." We meekly and quietly made our way to our chairs, sort of like kindergarten children filing back into a classroom after a fire drill.

Geoff's declaration about wasting his time was particularly poignant, though few if any of us in the room realized it at the time. Geoff Nightingale had cancer, and died within the next year.

The Meeting Dance

The meeting dance is more exotic than the Brazilian Samba. It is more frenzied than the Cuban Rumba. It is more deadly to an organization than the venomous Black Mamba. You get the alliterative point.

It begins with a precise meeting time, usually at the top of the hour or on the half hour. A few people timidly gather around the conference table. One person pokes his head in the door, coughs like a cat with a fur ball to get attention, and then quickly retreats, realizing that not all people are present. Then, in turn, another person currently at the table, in one fluid and exquisite move gets up, does a slight curtsy and slowly strolls out the door, usually leaving a pen and paper on the table, a sign he or she will return. This is repeated to the tune of the Virginia Waltz for 15 or 20 minutes, when, quite by accident, all arrive at the same place at approximately the same time. Then, of course, someone's cell phone rings.

The basics of a good meeting never change, sort of like a pair of argyle socks that stay on those stinky feet until the home team's winning streak ends. It is made up of an objective and an agenda on how to get there. Nothing more elaborate. Slides, advanced computer graphics, gee-whiz video equipment are all fluffy add-ons, and generally do no more to move the agenda than add noise. They won't hurt, but they are probably not needed, at least to the extent they are used today.

You probably thought these paragraphs were about lateness; which, to an extent they are, but they really have more to do with the wasting of time, and tardiness is merely one manifestation of its collateral damage.

When you reach age 40, you begin thinking about your own mortality. When you reach the 50 marker, you find yourself grabbing the *Economist* magazine, and turning first to the obituary page, the publications own cemetery for the famous and infamous. At 60, you are in the Yellow Leaf period, quickly heading to that Noble Rot stage. At this point, you are selfishly protective of every gulp of breath. This is not a bad thing.

A few years back I wrote a book called "The Portfolio Bubble: Surviving Professionally at 60". It was all about making the most of one's time, sort of like a metaphorical Heimlich maneuver for those of us who believe work life doesn't end when the first grandchild comes along. While recognizing that Sun City, big three-wheelers and shuffleboard courts are fine for a large segment of the population, others of us would rather suck down a soda pop with an arsenic chaser than retire.

Until I was almost 50, I could sit and watch automobiles race around a circle via a television screen for half of a Sunday afternoon.

I could take in a movie that I knew to be mediocre just for the sake of munching on a big box of popcorn, and I could watch big boys play little boys games such as baseball, realizing perfectly well that a single game in a 160 game plus schedule probably won't make a whole lot of difference in my life. It was interesting to watch Barry Bonds clobber another ball over the fence, and, interesting I guess as to whether he was on steroids when he broke the home run record. Frankly, it will not materially affect my life one way or the other. Or yours, unless you work for NASCAR or you are the commissioner of baseball.

Don't get me wrong. There is nothing I would like better than to be in the stands behind the third-base line, watching my Atlanta Braves. Going to see a Darlington 500 NASCAR race, and even serving as a member of a pit crew, was the thrill of a lifetime. And I believe movies are great entertainment and have a lot to teach about life.

However, as one gets a little older, he or she is increasingly worried about being what I call "late for life". We need to show up for the things we really enjoy, and tune out the humdrum. There is a certain selfishness quotient here, but go ahead, pamper yourself. Take out a piece of paper and write down the things that suck up time, but are truly rewarding to you. Call it your Time Bible, and stick to it.

Advertising and PR Awards: That Phony, Make Believe World

So much for my discourse on time. Next, let's take the most innocuous of my list of sorrows – advertising awards. I don't like them. I think most are phony.

I once won an award for thinking about writing a newspaper series on mental health. Somewhere in a box is a wooden plaque that actually says The Hillsborough County Mental Health

Communicator Award for 1969. Thus, with nary a word put on paper, I became an AWARD WINNING reporter for *The Tampa Times*, the last paper in the U.S. to go from a nickel to a dime, and then – as with most afternoon newspapers – it promptly folded. By that time, however, I had moved on to win awards at various other newspapers for, in essence, doing a job. We live in an award-happy world, and the advertising business is no exception. Awards are given for breathing.

During a seven-year stretch in the 1980s, my little agency in Charleston, West Virginia won Best of Show in the Tri-State Area (West Virginia, Kentucky and Ohio) five times, collecting a closet full of glass, brass and wood in various phallic shapes. Today, several moves later, I have no idea where this menagerie might be, though perhaps some of the trinkets are tucked away in the same box as the Hillsborough County Communicator Award.

I have no use for them. They can't be eaten, nor can they be pawned for more than a few kopeks. The plaques, one could suppose, might serve as good, solid roofing material, and the more exotic shapes perhaps could be used to ward off evil spirits if properly inspired. In a post-Apocalyptic 22nd century, they could be attached to sticks and used as weapons.

Some folks might have a hard time understanding this. However, coming across my desk each week are entry forms for dozens of advertising and public relations contests. They all offer fame, but, sadly, no fortune. They do, however, cost a fortune to enter. They all, of course, are "prestigious". They are called by their nicknames, and I exaggerate only slightly here: Opies, Eddies, Louies, Johnnys, Bettys, and so forth. Certainly, receiving them causes momentary elation, like the sugar delivery system of cotton candy.

However, one soon realizes that winning first place for a 30-second television production in the category of retail foods having to do with chocolates that come in red wrappers and are sold on the bottom shelf at the Kroger market is a rather restrictive category. Again I exaggerate, but the last awards ceremony flyer that was sent to me had no less than 30 first place categories, and then you have second and third places and, of course, honorable mention. Talk about shooting fish in a barrel.

Recently, I was told about an awards contest publicized by a Ukrainian business magazine, in which the word went out that first place had already been purchased, but that second and third places were still available. The story might not be true, but it is illustrative in a country named on the all-time corruption hit parade.

Clients want results. So-called creativity is a Lucky Strike extra.

I am reminded of a client observation I recently read: "You can walk through advertising agencies and see all kinds of awards on the wall," he said. "But what I would really like to see is a framed and attractive graph showing my product increasing in sales."

And then there is this comment from James Harralson, a one-time CEO of Royal Crown Cola:

"In the past, we have had a strategy, but our agencies didn't stick to it. But they did make good commercials and they did win awards. This may surprise you, though. I don't care about awards; I want to sell product."

Language Fraud: Or F-You, F-Off, and Other Pleasantries

My last list of sorrows – sometimes they are referred to as pet peeves or maybe just the grumbling of the aged – has to do with language, in this case the English language as often spoken in business.

I remember a time when the F-word was for failure in school. In addition, on rare occasions, it was used as the absolute nuclear meltdown obscenity when every other expletive seemed to have the impact of marshmallows thrown against a wall.

Today, it is fairly well common in verbal business, and in every occupation. That's okay. It is a solid Anglo-Saxon word made popular by leading ladies who appear in almost the same type of romantic comedies in which Doris Day acted in yesteryear. Only she said, "Aw, fudge."

Since the word has received institutional status and most likely is even used by your blue-haired grandmother on occasion, there are more business terms I find more vulgar, those that I place in the category of language fraud. These are generally terms that have one meaning for the person uttering them, and quite another for the person on the receiving end. But first, let's examine the F-Word, quaintly.

The first time I actually heard a woman say the F-word was in 1970 or thereabouts – the Vietnam War was going strong, and I was asked by my news service to do a story on an underground newspaper, this one near the U.S. Army's Fort Campbell on the Tennessee-Kentucky border. I was shocked.

To write those three words today seems so decadent, so naïve, so totally sheltered – but I wasn't. I had already earned my reporting stripes covering civil rights riots in America's south and unearthing slum-housing scams in Tampa, Florida. The young lady editor who made the remark, rather casually in referring to the war, wore faded Levi's, a khaki shirt and white, low-topped tennis shoes. She had long blonde hair, not willowy, but straight, and wore no lipstick. She had a thin mouth, and a wry and defiant smile. She was cute, but by no means beautiful. Want me to tell you more, maybe what perfume she wore? I believe it was a rather decadent Shalimar. Such was the impact of a lady saying the F-word, something today that is common on multi-channeled cable television.

Late night talk show hosts interviewing guests are known to

joke about the possibility of four-letter words being beeped out. The Washington Post in late June 2004 used it on its pages for only the fourth time in the history of the newspaper, though numerous times it has dealt in euphemisms such as "he used a vulgar expletive for intercourse" or as in "F_ _ _", or occasionally, "F-You."

Sen. John Kerry, the former Democrat presidential candidate, used the word in Rolling Stone Magazine when running for president of the United States. Vice President Dick Cheney uttered the expletive, I assume as an action verb, when he suggested on the U.S. Senate floor, of all places, that Sen. Pat Leahy "F-off."

The Senate, for those of you who are not that familiar, is a place where people refer to one another with comity and superlatives, no matter how much they would like to put the other's head in a meat grinder. The practice goes back more than 200 years.

The exchange between the vice president and Leahy, a nut, berries, and environmental senator from Vermont, caused somewhat of a mini-scandal, though in terms of hurricane strength scarcely turn a leaf in the vice presidential bluster.

My own view of the use of the F-word is obviously complex. As I grew in the newspaper/wire service business, I began to learn that the obscenity was one of the 20 or so basic words in the journalist's everyday language. Balance this with a Southern Baptist upbringing in which the word 'hell' could only be used in a biblical context, and the picture becomes a little confused. Still, I generally only use it with the guys and occasionally with a female executive assistant who is witness to all my intemperate eruptions. I never recall using it with the first Ms. Willard, the second Ms. Willard, or for that matter, the third Ms. Willard. I have never used it or would use it around anyone's children, especially my own.

I joke that I allot myself 10 F-words a month, though I probably go over this meager allotment by dozens. And, truth be known, I thought it was kind of endearing when blue-eyed actress Cameron Diaz told a goofball Ben Stiller, "I'm just f - - -g with you" at the sweet conclusion of the romantic comedy "There's Something About Mary".

Still, I am queasy of its use. It leaves the after taste of turpentine mouthwash, even when preceded by an pre-apology, such as, "Excuse me for using this word, but this guy is a real......" I find women sometimes take this tack a lot, particularly in Eastern Europe where it entered the vocabulary only a dozen or so years ago.

The F-word is just one in a series that seem to be part of everyday business life, and contributes very little to commercial discourse. Admittedly, it does have more impact than those silly "emoticons" some people use on e-mails. Maybe the problem with those icons is that there is not enough emotional range and an F-You icon should be added. I have no idea which form it would take, or even color. I would hope it wouldn't be too graphic.

All told, however, the word probably has more gutter elegance to it then when business people use language fraud such as, "what's the bottom line" and "all I want is a level playing field" – weasel phrases all.

A Cacophony of Clichés

The first time a new and clever phase or word is used it is like man discovering a new star among the glittering planets in the galaxy. It is colorful. It is insightful. It is, in fact, useful. Eventually, however, it is like every other pebble on the beach, but not nearly as colorful, as insightful or as useful as the tried, the true and the correct. It becomes plagiarism by the multitudes.

A Google search turns up more than 24 million written occasions where "all I want is a level playing field," is committed. The number tops 18 million for "at the end of the day". There are five million references to one of my all-time favorites, "what part of 'no' don't you understand", including a song title. "The bottom line", one of the most obvious written and verbal utterances, evidently is finally going out of favor. It clocked in at about nine million references. Others, such as, "Here's a quarter – Call someone who cares", (79,300 references) became an anachronism simply because pay telephone booths became antiques, replaced by the ubiquitous cell phone.

Let's face it: In global business, there literally should be no "end of the day", even metaphorically. What CEO really, in his heart of hearts, wants "a level playing field"? He might as well wander aimlessly around the business world with a sign on his back that says, "Kick Me". This "bottom line" thing is really confusing, particularly when used as "Let's get to the bottom line" or "The bottom line is". There is rarely a bottom line. There is always wiggle room. It has become a tissue paper gauntlet, tossed down at the beginning of debate, or as an absolute when in reality is a very subjective term.

Cliché City: Advertising

The advertising industry has given birth to thousands of cute slogans that once were as fresh as the Pillsbury doughboy but now are like week-old croissants. After 25-plus years, "Where's the beef?", the utterance of a little old lady named Clara Peller for Wendy's hamburgers still crops up on occasion, but apparently is suffering a generational death (there are only 108,000 mentions on Google). However, in 1984, former Vice President Walter Mondale used it in a debate against President Ronald Reagan in reference to the latter's alleged lack of a program. It didn't work. Mondale was swamped in the general election. So much for the transferal of commercial marketing to politics. Dipping back even further, it was common in the 1970s to quote Alka Seltzer's "I can't believe I ate the whole thing" (including some rather vulgar jokes), but today such an utterance would draw quizzical stares. In the 21st century,

Budweiser gave us "Wazzzzzzzzzzzzzzzup?" Thankfully, this lasted about as long as a Hollywood haircut.

Acronyms: Can We Buy A Vowel?

It is amazing how many people come up with strong, image-packed names for their companies and then truncate those jewels by reducing them to a couple of nondescript letters.

There is the maddening tendency by some – clients, vendors, and often our own people – to shorten The Willard Group to TWG. Granted, when most people think of Willard they think of a movie by the same name and thousands of rats running wild. There was also Frances Willard, the prohibitionist (the evidence suggests she was not even vaguely related to my immediate family), a company called Willard Batteries, and a plaintive song written by the late John Stewart, discussing "Willard, he's a loner..." Of course, there is the famous Willard Hotel in Washington, D.C., but my only connection there has been as a guest.

IBM can get away with being called IBM instead of International Business Machines because it has been around since Adam and Eve begat calculators. Few people under the age of 50 would even recognize the actual name. On the other hand, Hewlett-Packard these days is going by the initials HP, which dehumanizes what was a great company started in the garage of the curious Mr. Packard. This is a shame. Now the name sounds like a brand of motor additive.

At The End of The Day

"At the end of the day", we could go on forever never knowing "the bottom line" while we desperately seek "a level playing field". However, this is merely the "tip of the iceberg", and "at this point in time" we should move on to more clichés, several of the new ones I just introduced. Of the two last offending phrases, "tip of the iceberg" is merely trite. I find the latter reference to time so offensive that it causes me to break out in ugly hives, beat the kids and kick the dog.

A website with which I have some familiarity conducted a poll of its readers (5,000) and they voted "at the end of the day" the most irritating phrase that has crept into the English language. My personal preference (it came in second), the one that has the effect of fingernails across a chalkboard, is "at this point in time". I think it is the prevalence factor, as well as the fact it is used by so many supposedly learned persons who have alphabet degrees and talk like English butlers. For some reason, it is difficult for these scholars to realize that the last two words relating to time are about as necessary as adding Coca-Cola to Jack Daniels. One is simply language fraud and in bad taste while the other is sacrilege.

Frankly Speaking

There are a whole series of clichés that set you up for the proverbial fall, those often used by traveling medicine men and politicians. However, as I believe Will Rogers said, I repeat myself.

Back in the late 1950s, there was a television show called "Maverick", with the main character being Bret Maverick (actor James Garner), a wizened and charismatic card shark of the old West. While not remembering much from the series, I do remember the episode when the bad guy said to our hero, "Maverick, frankly I......" Frankly, I would be lying to you if I wrote that I remembered the remainder of the line, but that's just the point. Maverick answered back with a wry smile, "Well, my old pappy use to tell me that when ever anyone starts off a sentence with 'frankly', you can pretty much be assured he is going to lie to you."

There are certain truths that stuck with me through the ages. They were uttered by Davy Crockett, Ike Eisenhower, Bob Dylan, or the bully down the street, Mickey Morola, who was by far the biggest influence. They are all childhood nuggets, writ large. This time it was the drifter "Maverick", but his admonition has a lot of friendly cousins. One such is: "To tell you the truth, I...."

This one implies that the party on the receiving end of the conversation was born with an IQ approximating the number of big toes our species is thought to have. In this case, the speaker acknowledges from the outset he would not normally tell the truth, but in this particular instance, he was prepared to do you a favor. Another phrase, which closely rivals it, is that all-time hit parade favorite, "to be perfectly honest with you", most often used by salespersons wearing chartreuse-colored jackets.

The PR Business

In the public relations business you have a bushel full of strategies and tactics depending on mood, need and objectives. If someone is successful at applying them, he becomes a "guru" or maybe a "maven". At some point – I believe the early 1990s – "maven" took over from "guru" as the favored term for someone with a little expertise. In public relations, those who really romanced the English language began to address us gurus turned mavens by the whimsical term, "spin doctor" or even "spinmeister". Spin doctors, of course, were not really doctors who did things like brain surgery, but they engaged in that very uptown phrase, perception management.

However, it is not just in the PR world that a dizzying array of names and acronyms has taken over. The peddler of remedies, often branded self-help, is the modern day equivalent of the 18th century elixir salesman. He has a compound for every possibility. A recent book listed nearly 70 miracle cures, everything from one-minute management to total quality control as branded remedies for all business ailments, including, I believe, lock jaw and athlete's foot.

Minor Language Fraud

There are several terms, often related in some form to business, that crop up frequently. These are "blue-sky thinking" and "ballpark figure".

The first one, I confess, was really a puzzle the first time I heard it 20 years ago. I immediately pictured something more visual, more relaxing, and more beautiful than sitting in a stuffy conference room tossing ideas around. I soon learned that blue-sky thinking had less to do with the blue sky – or even for that matter thinking – than a contemplative 15 minutes in a shower or a walk in a park, both more conducive to thinking. Blue-sky thinking is, in essence, a forced march toward a creative solution. I don't recommend it for anyone, unless, of course, they wear combat boots. It tends to dumb down good ideas, rather than promote them.

"Ballpark figure", in terms of business, is a phase tossed out lightly for estimations that bear not the slightest resemblance to what will be the actual cost. Further, its first usage was probably by someone who had never seen the inside of a ballpark – I am assuming baseball here. These days, the interiors of baseball parks are actually a little smaller than in olden days to – one would assume – promote excitement with more home runs. Thus, to club one out of the old Cincinnati Riverfront stadium at centerfield you had to clobber it 420 feet. The new stadium, with the pretentious name of Great American Stadium, is 15 feet shorter. Therefore, the next time someone says they are going to give you the ballpark figure, ask which ballpark they have in mind.

Alas, there is also the incessant comparison to "it's not rocket science", as if rocket science were rocket science. After about 50 years of trying, we are just now tossing space junk within several thousand miles of Saturn. The most tangible things some believe to come from rocket travel are a few rocks from the moon and an orange-flavored drink called Tang. Compare this to something really difficult, such as filling out an Internal Revenue Service form.

Another term often used in business to spur creativity is "to think outside the box" or, as it is sometimes known, "to color outside the lines". What box? I have indicated to my colleagues that I want them thinking outside the box, around the box, in the box and on top of the box. I want them to create a new box. As to coloring outside the lines, the metaphor is a stretch, even for kindergarten kids who actually do color outside the lines. However these, like so many other sayings when first uttered, were like creative thunderbolts. Today they are as quaint as a 1950s rocker saying, "See you later alligator. After while, crocodile" (Which, by the way, in a nod to nostalgia, I say to my littlest daughter all the time).

Sometimes clichés appear which really are nonsensical, but are given credibility because they appeared in a movie, book or on the back of a cereal box. One is "pushing the envelope". You're a smart person. In the abstract, does that make sense to you – pushing an envelope? Why wouldn't we pull the envelope? Why wouldn't we just open the damn envelope? Or maybe put a stamp on it. But push the envelope? That makes absolutely no sense.

However, we all know from the movie and Tom Wolfe's book "The Right Stuff" in 1979 about the early astronauts and test pilots and that pushing the envelope meant to test the boundaries of most anything – endurance, taste, your wife. It fell into what I would call the cool lexicon, along with another cliché from the same book, "screw the pooch", which means to make a grievous mistake as it relates to aviation, generally, crashing. Actually – and this sort of takes us full circle – the original military term was F-the dog, meaning to goof off. As you can see, because we are squeamish about such things, we continue to bleep out the obscenity.

As the late columnist Dorothy Parker suggested about someone's acting talent, we have now run the gamut of clichés from A to B, realizing there are billions of others, and that, "at the end of the day" most will never be buried under what we all wish would be that proverbial "level playing field".

Chapter
15

The Phoenix Rises – Again

It seems I have veered to the right of my chronological account, hopefully not completely off the highway and into a ditch. However, in learning about my company and me, I think it is useful to observe beliefs and non-beliefs. Back to the story...

Revenge

I can be rather Faulknarian in character, which is to say, I am patient in awaiting revenge. It is true that revenge is a dish best served cold. This does not make me mean, even contrarian, merely human. When I received a late night phone call from Riva Levinson with the Burson-Marsteller owned BKSH one evening, I danced a jig in my living room.

It seems the powers that be were suggesting rather strongly that my nemesis in Burson's Emerging Markets practice, Mark D'Anastasio, resign. I wasn't told all the details. I was merely asked to take up where he was to leave off and in a hurry.

Riva was a friend from days gone by. We had worked together the year before on a contract with Viktor Pinchuk, a Ukrainian oligarch and son-in-law of the then-president, Leonid Kuchma. However, all I gathered from her was that Ken Reitz, at that time the chief operating officer of Burson, was very dissatisfied with D'Anastasio. In a later conversation, Reitz told me he felt we lost more than we gained with government projects. I didn't disagree.

Ironically, just a week before, I had issued a declaration in a neighborhood Brussels restaurant that I would eventually emerge the survivor in my corporate battles with Mark D'Anastasio. My audience was a group of senior Burson employees, and we were chilling out after preparations for region-wide media trainings scheduled the next day for Philip Morris. It was a moment of braggadocio that was propped up on whim and hope and nothing else. I was totally surprised by Riva's call, flabbergasted actually.

For about two years I had been discussing with Burson the possibility of opening a commercial office in Moscow, even though they had one at the time, and D'Anastasio was the presumed leader. The first request came from Jeff Hunt, a Texan who was leading Burson's efforts in Europe. I had also been approached about it in a telephone call from Kurt Kraus, another B-M executive, but who was located in New York. I felt something was in the air, but had no idea what.

This seemed to be my opportunity, though the immediate need was to troubleshoot a situation with a World Bank capital markets project with which Mark had been involved. I immediately got on the plane and met with the local Burson financial officer and the various members of the capital markets team. I also met with officials of the Russian government, and it became apparent this was not going to be an easy assignment. The main reason for the difficulty was Mark. He had forged relationships, and the government could not understand why he was being dumped. I could not tell them, primarily because I was not sure. I had been given no official explanation.

However, I moved forward with an intention to establish a Moscow office, taking baby steps to create a model I would later come to realize had no chance of working in the rough and tumble world of Russian public relations. I even sounded out Young & Rubicam's Yuri Pashin about using a small corner of his expansive domain in the World Trade Center. As the competitive situation was to develop a few years later, I am glad he did not take me up on my request.

The only way to enter Moscow is with both guns blazing, whole hog and with a missionary zeal that all will work out in the end. Tiptoeing was for sissies. To try to set up a faux office would have been a mistake. We eventually landed at the World Trade Center in Moscow, but not on Pashin's floor. We didn't hire willy-nilly, but as we obtained more and more business, we brought seasoned people on, including John Mann, a young African-American who had worked at an agency in Kazakhstan and Igor Kirilyuk, a topnotch PR guy from Coca-Cola public affairs in Ukraine.

In the public relations and ad business, it is difficult to keep people for whatever is considered a duration. You just have to be happy that you hired good people and they serve the company well. Mann later left to be an international spokesperson for Russian oligarch and Chelsea football club owner Roman Abramovich, while Kirilyuk eventually took a senior position with a Ukrainian metals company, MetInvest. I was proud of each graduate from Willard, but particularly those two.

In the first couple of days, I started interviewing possible candidates to run the office and enlisted the help of someone who was later to move from the category of colleague to very good friend, Roman Diukarev. Roman made several suggestions, and I interviewed each one, including Karina Grosheva, who I had hired for Burson several years earlier. However, Karina had already accepted a new position at Visa International.

Except for Karina, none seemed the right fit either in personality or work habits. I met them at the National Hotel, usually in the downstairs atrium restaurant, and generally the first thing out of their mouths was "what kind of a package are you offering?" They didn't care about the job so much as whether a company car, an expense account and four weeks vacation were included in the "package". I hated the word "package" when it came to benefits. I felt I was on the other side of a union negotiation. While I was hiring for a senior position in this instance, I once wrote down my **Top 10 suggestions for people seeking jobs.** I reconstruct them as best remembered for that grain of salt worth to which people are always referring:

1. I like people who are slightly weird, particularly in positions that require more than a measure of creativity – which is most positions. I don't mean loonytoons but creatively bizarre. In other words, I like idea machines. Show me in an interview how you can come up with that silver bullet idea. Yes, on the spot.

2. Demonstrate curiosity about my business that you want to become your business. Ask questions that show me you did your homework prior to the interview. Make me interested in you by showing how much you are interested in my business.

3. Don't tell me you were a straight "A" student in college. That says to me you probably didn't have much fun. Tell me you were a straight "A" student, worked 20 hours a week at a paying job, and still managed to climb on top of a bar called Craw Daddy's and sing Patsy Cline's Crazy one night a week.

4. Or, alternatively, tell me you were an average student, but held down that 20 hour a week job, and still managed to climb on top of a bar and sing Crazy three nights a week. In other words, show me you are interested in life.

5. Don't tell me what you think I want to hear. If you come gift wrapped, and I find the goods aren't there when the package is opened, I will be sorely disappointed.

6. Urge me to call your references. Dial the numbers if you wish. I will know you have already prepared them for my call, but I will appreciate the fact you are prepared and showed initiative. Don't, please don't, say, "References on request". I hate that. It just shows me you were too lazy to contact people in advance to solicit those testimonials.

7. Be truthful, even if it is painful. A good employer will never ask things that are personal and none of his or her business. However, your work history – if an investment is going to be made in you – is the potential employer's business.

8. Act like you really want the job. There is nothing more off-putting to an employer than the feeling that the person being interviewed considers you his second or third choice. This leaves the taste of moldy crackers and stale beer.

9. It's your interview too. A good employer will appreciate being grilled – in a kindly way – about the nature of the job, the benefits, the pay and the prospects for the future. This is your time to also ask "life and work" questions.

10. Dress for the job interview. It is your one shot. It isn't a fashion show, but the employer wants to know he or she is interviewing a serious candidate. The fact is, you can be weird and still wear a tie – at least at the interview.

Eventually, out of the blue, Roman asked me if I had thought of him for the Moscow office. Of course I had, but he seemed extremely happy freelancing, and had expressed this to me on various occasions. My answer was immediate: I would love to have him head up the new Moscow office of The Willard Group. There was no haggling over price. He stated a reasonable number, and I jumped at the opportunity.

I had recently worked with Roman on media and issues training in Romania. We had on several occasions worked with Romanian politicians, including the last prime minister, Calin Popescu-Tariceanu, as well as, on different trips, with various presidential candidates and members of government.

In life you have acquaintances, friends and those people you sincerely call non-blood brothers. In Ukraine, I had one, a fellow named Maxim Rylsky, an executive vice president in our company and one of the first people I met in 1994, and in Russia there was Diukarev. I first met Roman at the Apollo restaurant a few weeks after I landed in Kyiv. Y&R's Pashin, for whom he worked, accompanied him that evening. Pashin at the time was scouting Kyiv for a possible office site. The meeting was fortuitous in that 11 years later I would be engage in an epic struggle with this same Pashin with Roman on my side. At the time, I thought nothing of Y&R's long-range plans for an office. In my mind, I would only be in Ukraine a year.

In 30-plus years of hiring, bringing on Roman is the best decision I made. He is not only a good manager, but also one of the most strategic public relations experts in Eastern Europe. He has an innate ability to put a client at ease seemingly by gently rubbing his whiskers and being contemplative. While he talks the talk, he just as easily walks the walk, whether it is on crisis training or an actual crisis. If I were a client, he is the person I would want advising me, and on numerous occasions over the years I have sought out his advice.

In December 2001, we launched our Moscow office without fanfare. We had no clients, and merely the remnants of a fast-dying World Bank capital markets program that was to be out the door within 30 days. However, we had a foothold and a lot of determination.

Sergey Nosov, my previous driver in Moscow, quickly joined the small team and the two of us teamed up on new business. Sergey was always more than a driver and he showed it in that first six months. Our first public relations hire was Tonya Gerfanova of Samara, who, like many on the Moscow team, became good friends and remained so long after leaving Willard. She was later to join my former colleague Karina Grosheva at Visa International.

I interviewed Tonya in one of the oligarch suites at the National Hotel overlooking Red Square. I had arrived late the night before and because it was late and I had stayed at the hotel many times, a sympathetic night clerk gave me the corner suite at the cost of a regular room. It contained a palatial bedroom, living room and a sitting room. From that first meeting, Tonya might have gotten the impression we were a well-heeled company. She soon found out differently.

Throughout the winter, I whizzed back and forth between Moscow and Kyiv numerous times. Nosov would set up various new business meetings for me. At the time, "Dancing with the Bear: Crisis Management in Eastern Europe", had just come out, and I used that as a calling card. In each meeting, I acknowledged the obvious, that there was a public relations company virtually on very corner – "You can pick up a snowball and toss it in any direction and hit a PR company," I said, dozens of times. The difference in Willard, I added, was that we were leaving the arms and legs tactics to others and sticking to what we know and do best, the heavy lifting, the crisis work, the senior consulting and the strategic thinking. Truth was, we would do almost anything even vaguely related to PR.

In the meantime, Roman was handling the first real client to literally walk through the door, the beverage company then going by the name of Sun Interbrew. We were quickly on board, primarily offering senior counsel and helping the company's public affairs official, Irina Kibina, with day-to-day tasks as called upon. Often you find that clients met early become fast friends. Irina moved on to Evraz, the giant Russian steel company, and then to Sberbank, Russia's well-known state savings bank and then to TNK-British Petroleum.

Nosov and I were all over the city, from Siemens to Adidas, from McDonald's to British Airways, from Golden Telecom, to Kraft. It was a very cold winter with high snowdrifts, but here we were peddling a service, handing out books and leaving off information like a team of workhorses hooked to a wagon. The intensity of the effort was to pay off, and it took the Moscow office only six months to begin paying back the $60,000 or so invested. By comparison, we dropped $350,000 in Istanbul, and could never get it to pay off. As a matter of record, very few of the companies Nosov and I visited ended up being immediate clients, though some advised us to others that did become clients. I am convinced that this winter campaign, slogging through the elements, was crucial to the Moscow office's ability to survive and then to thrive. Additionally, with the publishing of *The Flak*, it gave us additional free press exposure, including a sizable article in the *Moscow Times* and an interview on the prestigious *Echo Moscow* radio, as well as numerous business publications.

Over the years, Roman has remained at the helm. I continued to give him greater responsibilities, making him president of public relations for the company in 2006. I have never felt any competition with Roman as to who is the PR guru and who is the metaphoric grasshopper. I think we are combinations of both. I might write the books, but Roman – by virtue of being on the hot seat in a very active capital city that is considered the center of the universe in Eastern Europe – probably has more practical experience in certain aspect of public relations. In any event, we made a good team. In our unofficial succession plan, he is at the top of the ladder.

Before long, the one remaining project on which Burson-Marsteller worked on in Russia, Yukos Oil, run out of a small office in Central Moscow by a half-dozen employees, withered. This was prior to one-time Yukos chief Mikhail Khodorkovsky being sent to a Siberian prison for, in essence, challenging the regime of President Vladimir Putin. The formal charge was tax evasion. Several of those on the account, as well as Sergey Nosov who had worked with me, eventually joined Khodorkovsky, working on charitable activities and media outreach.

The door was left wide open for a Burson-Marsteller/Willard affiliate relationship, one that should have been made in heaven given the vast experience the principals had in Burson culture and way of doing business. We were certainly not the biggest agency in Russia at less than 20 people, nor did we have the greatest billings. However, we ran a clean as a whistle operation, something that is rare in Moscow public relations where buying coverage is considered normal and avoiding taxes the rule.

The Moscow office was to see several business milestones that contributed greatly to building the office. The first was the city's effort to secure the 2012 Summer Olympics, the Olympics that went eventually to London. The other was a huge industrial development exhibition in Cannes, France in which we were hired by the region of Nizhny Novgorod to put its best foot forward. They were both multi-million dollar projects with Burson bringing Willard in on the Olympic bid and Willard bringing Burson in on the industrial development project. The latter was a resounding success in that a half-billion Euros in business was pledged. While the loss of the 2012 games to London was disappointing, Moscow did make it to the final five cities, which was significant in itself, and established the city as a player for a future Olympic bid.

During this time, the part of the business I really wanted to move forward, that of strategic counsel, was beginning to take off with such clients as Russian Railroad, Nestle, Russian Sberbank and Bunge. My trips to Moscow became less frequent as I concentrated more on developing Istanbul and keeping Kyiv running smoothly.

For much of the decade, we had a tenuous but suitable relationship with Burson-Marsteller. Both companies were joined together by the commercial necessity of doing business in Russia.

Burson, by and large, had failed on its own in the commercial sector during previous years, but had limited success on government funded work, depending on the stewardship and cost-effectiveness of the project.

As a rule, I think it is difficult for any multinational to navigate the Byzantine system in Russia. Goldman Sachs, the investment banker, entered the Russian market with fanfare three times, leaving twice. In my view, you have to have a hybrid of a company that combines values of the west with the realities of the east. In the past, Burson had toed the line with Western expatriates leading the charge. It never got into serious trouble, but it didn't make money either. My constant worry was that Burson would push Willard aside, tempted by a large Russian PR company that did business the "new" way of the East as opposed to the "old fashioned" way of the West.

Often we would get word that Burson was meeting with a Russian PR behemoth, and they were fairly upfront with us in saying we were small potatoes, that they could do bigger deals with the truly local PR companies. My recommendation to any multinational would be to take a longer view, and recognize that good corporate governance will take you further than teaming up for reasons based on instant gratification. However, it is difficult to resist the lure and promises of companies which promise to bring in a basketful of large Russia projects.

As I write this on September 16, 2008, greed has just led to the downfall of Lehman Brothers after 150 years and to the selling of another venerable giant, Merrill Lynch, to the Bank of America at 66 per cent of last year's value. Of course I am mixing apples and oranges, but that is not unusual in an increasingly volatile Wild East. In the United States, they call it a sub-prime crisis. I call it plain old greed. I also take loyalty seriously.

During this period I met with a longtime friend who had recently become chief operating officer of Burson-Marsteller, Rick Powell.

I had known Rick since my first year at Burson in Washington when he served as an assistant to the Washington president, Don Cogman. In 2007 and 2008 we met on several occasions in Kyiv where he was wrapping up a piece of business. In the latest meeting, he acknowledged that Jeremy Galbraith, the European president of Burson, most likely would move the company's allegiance from Willard to a large Russian firm. I told him it was a mistake, but acknowledged that the "train had probably already pulled out of the station." Frankly, at this point, I was tired of fighting with Y&R and WPP and I didn't necessarily want a disagreement with B-M. I only asked that he give us sufficient notice.

In fact, for a recent project – after being informed that Burson was teaming with the Russian company – we aligned for this one business opportunity with Brunswick, a respected London-based company, working with its New York office. We won the project for Russia and Ukraine. The fact is affiliation agreements had never stopped B-M or Willard from seeking other opportunities. B-M had chosen another firm for the U.S. Treasury's new currency launch, and we had worked through London-based MS&L for Western Union.

However, after a short meeting with Powell at Kyiv's Premier Palace hotel, I wrote Powell a note that read:

"Thanks for the drink and taking time to describe Burson-Marsteller's thoughts regarding both Moscow and Kyiv. I appreciate the heads up.

"As I noted, this is one train that apparently has pulled out of the station when it comes to Moscow. We are not happy given our long history with B-M and the fact that we were asked to go into Moscow by B-M in 2001. We started the office from scratch without a single B-M client and we grew it.

"I do understand Jeremy looking east and getting all starry-eyed.

It has happened before. Our advice to any Western company, which we give each week, is to be wary of Russian partners, or Ukrainian partners for that matter.

"We have seen big and little companies suffer because of it, from Telenor and Bunge, to the Western-owned saloon down the street. The fact is, your intended affiliate doesn't do business like we do in Moscow or Kyiv, or like you do in New York or London. However, I am not going to restate the arguments here. The history is there.

"We simply appreciate sufficient notice. We have our own suitors and want to position ourselves as well in any news release that might be issued in the future.

"As for Kyiv, I am happy to work anything out. We feel we were good stewards of B-M's money for many years, and, in fact saved it from losing the entire bundle. However, when Y&R and WPP attempted to put us out of business, all bets were off. We fight fair, but we do fight. And our deal was not with Burson at the time, but with Y&R and Burson since we were more an ad office than a PR one.

"As always, it was good to see you. I enjoy our friendship, and it has been a long friendship and will continue to be. I hope you have a good trip back. It is difficult being away from family. Best Regards, Mike"

I ended the note by suggesting that the B-M European president, Galbraith, was an example of "an innocent abroad" when it came to Eastern Europe and suggested that his version of loyalty was not the Burson-Marsteller of old I knew so well. I was speaking specifically of the B-M of Harold Burson, the founder, a man who I greatly admire and who once visited our team in Moscow.

The fact is I maintain a loyalty to old employers that would make the Lone Ranger's Tonto pale by comparison. Of all the multinational PR companies, I genuinely believe not one can approach Burson in its ability to handle and solve complex issues for clients. However, having been assimilated into the giant holding company, WPP, B-M lost some of its luster simply by becoming merely one horse in a giant stable.

The reference to money was client invoices outstanding when Willard purchased the Burson-Marsteller office in 1998, the same year that an economic crisis restricted money being repatriated. At some point – actually it should have come much sooner – we acknowledged to ourselves that we had done more than our duty in being stewards of outstanding debts. When Y&R and WPP attempted to put us out of business – by trying to take our clients and approaching our people while we still had affiliation agreements – we felt it ended any perceived obligation.

Loyalty is something I find lacking with many but certainly not all multinational companies. They talk a good game and hire human resources experts to suggest that they are just one, big happy family. They are not. They talk ad nauseum about corporate social responsibility but really don't give a fig except to check the list that says "did that."

When I worked in the U.S. Senate, my boss would bemoan it wasn't like the "old Senate". With the passing of Senators Jim Eastland, Jacob Javits, Richard Russell, Barry Goldwater, John Stennis, Henry "Scoop" Jackson and Everett Dirksen, Sen. Byrd would say the institution was honorable as always but the newcomers to it were less so.

That's a little the way I feel about business today. It's an honorable profession, but it's got some real stinkers in it.

Chapter
16

Mistakes, I've Made a Few, But Then Again...

Mistakes come with the territory. They are like the character in the Halloween movies, Jason: They are never really down and out for the count, but always come back to haunt you.

In a given day, you might make a half dozen mistakes – a compliment given not deserved, a scold administer but misplaced, an accounting gremlin gone unobserved, a piece of advice that missed its mark. Unless you confine yourself to your office, and sleep the day away, you will make mistakes. Most of the time, they have the relative impact of a flea on the back of a tick on the back of a great big dog – very little. One of my missives to my staff says that "mistakes are forgivable and competence teachable."

But occasionally a small agency makes what can best be described as a whopper of a mistake and you lose a great deal of money. Recently, during a long-distance video Skype call with an advertising class at James Madison University, I was asked what my greatest failure was in business the last 10 years. That's easy – opening an Istanbul office.

I am not sure where I got the idea to open an office in Istanbul. While others were racing pell-mell to set up offices in other parts of Eastern Europe and even in the Central Asian republics, I looked to the south. I had always liked Istanbul and visited at every chance. However, sitting in a café overlooking the Bosporus and drinking sugary Turkish coffee, I had a vision that would turn into a nightmare. In this particular conversation, I was talking with a tour guide that came with the car and driver I had rented for the day to get around the city. I didn't particularly need the tour guide, and really wasn't utilizing his services. However, Mustafa was a good conversationalist and we spent the better part of three hours in the café while my then-wife was doing what she does very well, shopping in one of Istanbul's mega malls.

About the mid-point in this marathon session, it came to me; I don't know where from, maybe from a tiny little disembodied voice. Go against the flow. Open an office in Turkey while others flood to places like Almaty in Kazakhstan. It would be brilliant. After all, Almaty was a six-hour plane ride, while Istanbul was an easy one and a half from Kyiv. The logic seemed irrefutable. It was almost as close as Moscow. When I finally met my wife later that day, I told her of my idea. She thought it was wonderful.

That should have been a clue. Tanya had been totally against the Moscow office, suggesting that I was merely bringing trouble on myself. The Moscow office, under Roman Diukarev, had been a success. I looked like Einstein with Moscow.

Once the decision was made, I shared it with a few others. They were boosters, not a naysayer among them. It was only after we had sunk $350,000 in it without the first lira coming back that the boo birds came out. I have many faults, but one is staying too long at the party, holding on to a losing hand until the chips have already been taken from the table. If I had been born early enough and fought on the Japanese side in World War II, I would be one of those old soldiers that stayed hidden in a Philippine jungle until 1991. "Never give up" is my credo. And that can be really stupid.

Diukarev has always been one to want to open new offices, but his vision was more toward Almaty, St. Petersburg, Russia or even

Krasnodar, the fast-growing southern area of Russia near the Black Sea. However, he never raised a red flag over Istanbul; but, to his credit, he never jeered the home team and manager in defeat. David Payne, my partner for advertising, seemed to think it was a good idea at the time, but he saved his most critical remarks for a couple of weeks after I dissolved the partnership. I don't blame him. As for my brother Glen, I believe he felt I should have cut Istanbul loose long before I restricted our losses by cutting it to a skeletal staff.

Businesses set up in Istanbul every day, and many do succeed. There is no magic to running a business, though I think it does take talent and extraordinary drive to run one well. If I were to put myself on the couch and look into Freud's eyes, I can probably come up with several believable reasons we failed, or, as Gen. Custer probably would have said if he hadn't had a half dozen arrows sticking out of him: I failed.

The truth was I didn't know Turkey. While my first trip to the country was in 1968 as a young reporter covering a NATO exercise, and my second trip was a decade later to accompany my boss to a meeting with the prime minister, I was clueless about doing business in Turkey. We would have done just as well setting up an office in the Taliban-held sections of Afghanistan.

Turkey has this Disney-esque business atmosphere where folks in my profession were paid fairly well, but the clients expected service that could never possibly cover the costs. We were paying people in Turkey the same as in Moscow – the most expensive city in the world – and were working for penny-ante retainers that would have brought three times the fees in Russia, and at least two times the fees in Ukraine. For one beer company we work with six brands for less than $1,000 a brand.

I should have smelled a rat. I must have smelled some sugary aroma from the Spice Bazaar that enticed me, for I held on in that wonderful city for two years longer than I should have. I still love

Turkey – and in 2007 purchased a townhouse near the Mediterranean in Side, Turkey – but it is like the goddess that seduces you, and then abandons you.

After I had my near vision of a commercial utopia in Istanbul, I met with Roman in Moscow to sound him out on ideas of possible leadership for the office and what exactly did we hope to accomplish. I had learned from the Moscow experience that a powder-puff entry into the market was foolish. You couldn't put a toe in. You had to dive in headfirst and hope the pool was not too shallow. He suggested we talk to Sevda Erensel, who was deputy managing director of Capital PR, an affiliate of Burson-Marsteller, to get her opinion. On a trip to Istanbul where we had at least one client doing business in Ukraine, I had stopped by to see her.

In essence, Sevda made the suggestion Roman had made several years earlier. "Why not me?" she asked.

Sevda had gone to all the right schools in Istanbul. Her grandfather had been a doctor to Kemal Ataturk, the iconic founder of the Turkish Republic. When we went out to dinner, it seemed everyone in business in Istanbul knew her, and came up to our table. For the right price, she seemed a perfect fit. She exuded confidence in her own abilities to draw in business. We hired her and opened an office in the Tesvikiya section of downtown Istanbul, across from a Mosque and in an area of fashionable boutiques.

To this day, even with the struggle, I feel Sevda was the best person for the job, even though there were times I became frustrated with her. I was accustomed to a slightly more demure female lead. I was accustomed to Annie Oakley; she was Calamity Jane. She could cuss, drink and let loose off-color remarks with a would-be client as if one of the boys. To some it was endearing but to others I was told by Turkish businessmen it was off-putting. They were accustomed to a more gentile and demur Turkish lady. My view was it cut both ways, and you can't stifle a genuine personality. However, there was a more troubling aspect.

As much confidence as I had in Roman Diukarev, I still spent the winner of 2001 trudging through the snow, virtually going door to door to drum up new business. We worked as a team. That didn't happen in Istanbul. I would urge our small Istanbul staff to set up new business meetings for me when I arrived since they were in a better position to arrange them. I had never been a stranger to cold calls. However, it wasn't until late in the game that they actually succeeded in doing this, and by then it was too late. My assistant in Kyiv arranged many of my meetings in Istanbul.

They did set up numerous newspaper and magazine interviews for me. We got publicity, but not new business. I owned the company, but I felt my trips to Istanbul were an inconvenience, not to me but to the Istanbul staff. After a while, I mistakenly turned the lead over to Sevda, repeating over and over to myself that she must know what she was doing, and we would soon turn the corner. We never did, though there was a time we came close.

In the second year, Sevda had several personal tragedies. Just when it seemed we were about to break out of the box, her cousin, Genco Erensel, died of a heart attack on the way to work at the Willard office. He was only 29, and it was a shock. I received the call from another employee, Tijen Kundak, who broke the news over the telephone through sobs. He had died on the street just outside our office building. He was like a son to Sevda.

Genco was quiet and gregarious at the same time. He had this infectious puppy dog personality, even though he was tall and as bald as Mr. Clean. People warmed up to him within a moment of meeting him and I felt he had the potential to be a star in the business. Not long thereafter, Sevda's mother had a serious stroke that left her comatose.

This was the year we would like to remember to forget but couldn't. Overhead seems never to stop for personal tragedies, and Sevda, though devastated, soldiered on. During this time, the two of us probably became closer. I could empathize and sympathize with her even as I saw the business was at a standstill.

Genco had been an important part of our business with Efes, a beer company and our largest of four retainer clients in Turkey. He was out on the frontlines, overseeing the near nightly beer promotions. With him gone, we had lost the go-to guy, the single fellow who had the drive to work all day and then go to a promotion in the evening. I still have flashbacks of Genco and the limited time I spent with him. They are all good memories stored away.

I don't blame Sevda for Istanbul never getting its running legs. And, as noted earlier, I don't even regret bringing her on to lead the office. The failures began and ended with me not having sufficient knowledge of the Turkish market. With both Kyiv and Moscow, there was an incubation period in the cocoon of Burson-Marsteller. With Istanbul, there was no learning curve, and I delegated too much when I should have taken over and spent more time there. We still maintain a small Istanbul office and, ironically, this was Sevda's suggestion from the beginning. We are also making money, but we have diminished expectations.

However, it wasn't the best time in my life. On the very day I went to Istanbul to finalize the office, my wife was packing up to leave the apartment we had shared with our two children for the better part of seven years. It did not come as a surprise, and by this time, I wanted a separation as much as she. But in a chapter on mistakes, and in true confessional fashion, I include this here for personal catharsis – certainly not any plea for redemption. It is also part of the story.

If into everyone's life some rain must fall, this was a gully-washer of a storm. The story began six months earlier, on a day that should have been one of the high points in my life. We had just picked up my son Rob, a hip-hop singer who went by the name of *"Life the Guardian"*, at the Borispol airport. Other than visiting me, he was to appear at several nightclubs, and on television and radio shows. I had a crew shooting a video of his arrival and would do a short clip on him to run during his performances on large, plasma screens.

On the drive to the airport, and the wait at the VIP terminal, Tanya was standoffish. She had been that way, though, for days. While she also worked in the business as director of public relations, we were like strangers in the evening when we got home. She would go to her office and watch television, and I would go to mine where I also had my painting studio. We had settled into a comfortable but nearly separate existence.

Months earlier, she had learned to drive, taught by a young man in our PR department. When she was sufficiently accomplished, we bought a yellow Audi A3, a nice but small car. At the time, I still depended on my driver to take me to and from work, to appointments and generally about town, and so never drove the new car. It was her car. On weekends, she would be gone for hours at a time. She said she was practicing driving, and that this was her time. We led different lives, with the exception of working in the same office.

I don't know why Tanya, who was 20 years younger than I, decided on this particular day to burst my bubble. It could be that she felt she had to after I confronted her about why she seemed so unhappy. I had slipped into her office while Rob was unpacking and posed what I thought was a simple, uncomplicated question.

For about 30 minutes she told me that she was no longer in love with me, and suggested I had never been in love with her. She said she deserved better, and brought up every minor and major transgression over the previous nine plus years, from an argument I had had with our driver months before to the fact she hated living in Moscow eight years earlier when I could not put her to work in Burson-Marsteller. She said I was arrogant. While many adjectives have been used to describe my character over the years, this was one that seemed pulled from the stratosphere. Donald Trump is arrogant. I perhaps am obnoxious at times.

On the question of whether she deserved better, I don't argue. I plead no contest, and frankly don't feel putting up a defense is really needed. Life happens. However, I did ask for a second chance to improve whatever it was that she didn't like about me. In my view, she was probably right about many things. I had concentrated so much energy to the business and writing books and painting I had not spent enough time with my family. In a later life, I was to change this, not by curtailing those activities I loved, but merely by rearranging the furniture a little.

She agreed to a six-month trial period to see if we could recapture what we had if, indeed, we had ever had that much. I at least pretended that we did, for why else would someone live together and raise two children? I was serious about this six-month period. She was very skeptical, and kept referring to my public relations skills – indicating my ability to spin might be in high gear. My objective view of things was that I just needed to re-order my priorities. How wrong I was. Those six months were the worst of my life.

Immediately after the Titanic hit the iceberg, I, along with Rob and six-year-old Mia walked downtown to check out the Pa Ti Pa nightclub, where Life the Guardian would be performing in a week. We had lined up a rather well-known band to accompany him, and they were to practice over the next five days. However, I was in a fog. I couldn't concentrate where I was walking, much less make intelligent conversation. We were to stop and get Mia something for lunch, and I completely forgot about it. I was having one of those out-of-body experiences where something that is happening to you really can't be happening to you because you are not you but some stranger who you really don't care to meet.

Somehow, someway, we got through the week. Rob played to packed houses at two nightclubs, putting on energetic performances. At Pa-Ti-Pa, Tanya and I, along with Masha, then 14, had a VIP room overlooking the dance floor. For a while, it almost was as if the situation were normal. It wasn't. But, what the heck, it was merely another mountain to climb and I would do it like I had done everything else, putting one foot in front of the other. I had every confidence I could save the relationship. I didn't know she was already out the door and that this ghostly apparition had been left behind.

Rob went back to America the next week, and I got serious about saving the marriage. For two months I wrote a poem a day to Tanya, the quality of which was certainly suspect but I figured it was the thought that counted. Each day I would either email it to her, or leave it in a conspicuous place. After a while, it became the first thing I would do when I arrive early for work. In a way, it was therapeutic, and at least I thought I was making some progress. On weekends I would go out and buy flowers, for that was obviously one area I had neglected throughout our marriage – the little things. Tanya had accused me of having my driver pick out flowers for her when she was in the hospital after giving birth to Mia.

She was wrong. I picked the damned things out myself. I think they were roses. At least they were pinkish.

Chapter
17

Survival of the Fittest

This drama took place in April 2005. For my birthday the second week in May, we had planned a trip to London. It was here I thought, after all the flowers, after all the poems, after all the compliments; she would capitulate over a nice French dinner at our favorite restaurant in the West End, Mon Plaisir. Everything went mostly as to plan, with the exception that no heart melted and Tanya obliterated my personal Maginot Line, cutting through it like it was peanut butter and jelly.

We had a suite at our usual hotel, the Marlborough, and had taken in a musical at the Shaftsbury Theater prior to a late dinner. It could have been a sign that the play, which had just opened, had less time to run than our marriage. We did the scripted French restaurant and began the walk back to the hotel. I carefully broached the matter of our letting bygones be bygones for I was, I said, a changed man; and, after all, it was my birthday, a star-studded decade-beginning occasion. It was number 60. She implied that one doesn't change so quickly and that my track record wasn't very good.

While not defending myself – I think it would be ungentlemanly in this one-sided narrative – I would like to plead extenuating circumstances. Building a business and a life in Eastern Europe is no easy task, even in the best of times. Ukraine was in the middle of political turmoil, and foreign investment into the country was miniscule. My day usually began at 5 a.m. and didn't end until mid-evening, and then there were the weekend tasks of catching up on what I didn't get done through the week.

When we finally got back to the hotel, Tanya gave me my birthday present, which is not exactly the birthday present I was counting on. It was a handheld computer-telephone, a Nokia Communicator. It was a nice gift and certainly fit my modus operandi as being a fellow who likes to work most all the time, even while on a short holiday to London. So, you can see, unable to disguise the truth, I played into her hands. I loved the present.

By this time, however, what had been a quiet truce ended in an acrimonious argument as I put my new work toy aside. She went immediately to bed, and I slept a little on the couch in the adjoining room before getting back up. Mostly, I figured out how to work my Communicator and got little or no sleep. I also dug deep into the mini-bar. Very deep.

Even in London I had continued to demonstrate my affection through poems. Prior to leaving for England, I went on a writing frenzy and had prepared four poems in advance, one to leave for her in the bathroom for every day we were there. She read them, but said little. Over a 60-poem blitzkrieg, some were allegorical, others whimsy, a few maudlin or worse, and others just plain corny. There was one I sort of liked, for sometimes I dispatched the immediate problem from my mind, and wrote something I felt was more about me.

The Pink Rhino

He was relaxed, you might say,
In his velvet cocoon so comfy,
But along came a pink Rhinoceros,
And he went, well, Humpty-Dumpty.

That rhino was not a person,
Or even a thing I ought to say,
But it did have a horn for sure,
And it wasn't there for play.

Mystical and mysterious,
It was more an elaborate allegory,
Stumbling through the living room,
That's the truth. Sticking to my story.

Heard of the bull in the china shop?
Then picture a rhino on the loose,
Snorting and roaring, and finally goring,
That's right my friend, cooked my goose.

He felt his choices very limited,
No clue how long the rhino would stay,
Once a pink rhino is let loose on you,
Sure as life, it's darn difficult to slay.

He waited long for it to disappear,
Leave my home, he shouted out in fear,
But that rhino just stared as if to dare,
About his happiness?
That damn old rhino just didn't care.

Finally, in hopeless, dark desperation,
Said this rhino will have no gratification,
For he would exorcise it from his mind,
Think of something else, most all the time.

At this he was fairly successful at times,
There was intermittent peace in his rhymes,
The war of the roses was delayed for sure,
Though the topic was always the matter de jour.

Difficult to say if this story ends happily,
For some would say so corny, so daft,
But seems the pink rhino has taken leave,
In its place, a very large, blue giraffe.

I was shameless in painting goofy psychological pictures of what was and what might have been.

The following late August we were to vacation with the children in Brighton, England. In our short London trip we had scouted hotels and even made reservations. However, after terrorist bombs went off on buses in London, Tanya would have nothing to do with this particular vacation island, particularly when she learned the hotel we would be staying at had been bombed years earlier.

Even though I assured her the chances of being in the vicinity of a terrorist were about the same as winning the billion-dollar lottery but losing the ticket, she was still not calmed. So, we opted for the coast of Spain, not far from Barcelona in what was the most expensive 10 days of my life. I would have given the same amount of money not to have taken the vacation if I had known then what I was to learn just into the vacation. I would have preferred a vacation to Alcatraz, before they closed the prison.

For some reason I felt the family that vacations together stays together, and that to have a good time you have to spend tons of money on hotel suites and bring back loads of things you absolutely don't need. A day or two into the vacation, I knew I had made a big mistake. We were like two separate families; Tanya with the children and me with me, and maybe an alter ego or two. I was the tag-along, the fellow who hung outside the dozens of tourist shops holding the collected goods. I felt like a horse at a hitching post, and my saddlebags were loaded. Eventually, we would stop at one of the seaside cafés and have dinner. Hardly a word was said. We were on different planets.

During this time, I put the Communicator I had received as a birthday present three months earlier to good use. I touched base with friends around the world, even selfishly drawing them into the drama. People such as Lynn Wilson, a friend I remembered from high school because she was so darn smart, but hadn't seen since we were both 18. We had recently touched based as our high school class was planning a 40th reunion. Though work prevented me from attending, I had sponsored a classmate in Alaska who didn't have the money to fly to Pigeon Forge, Tennessee. I figured that he had been more popular then me anyway in school, and that I wouldn't be missed. Lynn was a one-time engineer for British Petroleum and at that time was working for the company in human resources. Her e-mails broke up the boredom, and I admired her from afar. She was and is a long-distance runner and was one of BP's first female engineers.

Another person was Patty Kerchner, my former assistant in Sen. Byrd's office, who had always been a close confidante when I worked with the leader. We had recently been back in touch. I had given her away at her wedding, but now she was divorced. Patty said, "Let me be the angel on your shoulder", which was touching.

I reached out to people, which in some ways was fairly pitiful and weak. However, the e-mails and text messages that zinged back and forth as I stood at the curb waiting for my family was much better and less expensive than therapy. I also was in contact with my former wife, Becky, who was always my closest friend, and that was obviously just one of the problems in my then current marriage.

After the speechless seaside dinner and after the shopping, we would generally land at an outdoor café and order exotic drinks. Masha was getting to the age she could at least taste the less potent versions.

Toward the end of the vacation, I got tired of it all. One night I just bolted up from my café seat, saying only that I "can't do this anymore", and walked alone the 30 minutes back to the hotel in another part of the city. "Can't do what?" I asked myself on the way back. I was unsure. Tanya called the bit of melodrama more PR. I started to hate the word, and I felt she was dispensing cruel and unusual punishment in drips, as if it were coming from a plasma bag.

On the next-to-last day of a rather surreal vacation, we chartered a car and driver and drove into Barcelona, one of the most beautiful and interesting cities in the world. Tanya asked that she and the kids be let out at a shopping center – a mall for Christ's sake – to shop at the same branded shops we had in Kyiv. We paid $500 for a car and driver so she could simply visit a mall. I, however, hijacked the driver and took a tour of the city, where I fell in love with the curiously wonderful architecture of Antoni Gaudi. I kept thinking that while Mia was still very young, Masha would learn from and enjoy knowing more about one of Europe's most interesting cities. As it was, she saw Barcelona through the prism of a shopping mall. Her Gaudi was a Ralph Lauren store.

By this time, I was thinking about a business trip I had taken to Norway a month earlier to visit with client Telenor. Roman Diukarev had made the same trip, and, as my best friend, was quite aware of my romantic malaise. We had skipped an unnecessary meeting and had taken a tourist boat on the fjord where he suggested that, as Sen. Byrd use to sing and play his fiddle, "there are more pretty girls than one." As we bobbed up and down on the inky black fjord, Diukarev suggested that I handicap future mates. I started with Cameron Diaz, but he said that wasn't very realistic. She wasn't in Eastern Europe. He suggested a lovely Russian who, at the time, was single and rather rich. I said she was certainly worth considering. It was all rather sexist conversation, though harmless, but it pointed out that I already was considering Mr. and Mrs. Willard in the past tense.

On returning to Kyiv, I was no longer convinced, to misquote Faulkner, that "when the last ding-dong of doom has clanged and faded from the last worthless rock hanging tide-less in the last red and dying evening" that I would not only endure, I would prevail. I would do neither.

In the final analysis, Tanya and I never crashed and burned. We were simple a soufflé that had gone flat. It ended with the sound of air going out of tires.

Chapter
18

Revival of the Fittest

It had been a traumatic year. I had finished next-to-last in my fantasy baseball league – even though Sammy Sosa was in my lineup – and my wife had left me for whatever reason.

It was soon to surface that a man-child who worked for me in our public relations group was a contributing factor. It seems that the two of them had been plotting to set up their own public relations business, and that my wife had already arranged to rent an apartment in another area of the city. Evidently on those driving lessons the two had become what I shall euphemistically describe as soul mates. This is not something; however, I would know when I went to Istanbul the day my wife was deciding what furniture to remove from our apartment and to – with my permission – clean out the safe so she would have a grubstake to start life in a cruel world.

I was a sap. I was Rick Blaine from the movie Casablanca, waiting on the Paris train platform with a dopey look on my face for the girl who got away. Doubly so because I had encouraged Tanya to take driving lessons from this string bean employee whom I never considered a threat. He was the fellow who would be playing games on his computer when I happened to walk by and would immediately and awkwardly hit an escape key and pretend to work. He was the substitute at the end of the bench who rarely got into the game, and when he did, it was in right field because he could no little harm there. For goodness sakes, I hired him as a favor to his father, a long-time acquaintance. He was fresh out of school at the time. He was an imbecile in waiting to become a full-fledged idiot.

But I didn't know all this when I boarded a plane to Istanbul that Monday morning for a business trip that would launch my new life. I felt relieved, even liberated that it was all over. It was not a sudden break, but a six-month ordeal I had just completed. It was the marital version of a stint at the Marine training camp at Parris Island. It was brutal and I felt the life had been sucked out of me.

We had been separated for six months, even though we lived under the same roof, even sleeping in the same bed but on extreme opposite sides. On the plane, I wondered what it would feel like when I returned to Kyiv in two days, giving Tanya sufficient time to move her life away from me. Would I walk through the apartment and picture Mia at her computer, or Masha watching MTV? What would I change about the place to rid it of memories, some good – mostly good?

I went through multiple meetings that day, an interview at a popular Turkish newspaper, a meeting with the CEO of a condiment manufacturer and a tour of the office we had just acquired. That evening, Sevda Erensel, my Istanbul manager, and I had a drink at the landmark Pera Palais Hotel, where Agatha Christie wrote *Murder on the Orient Express*. I had stayed there with Tanya on one occasion, in a suite that had been used by a former president of the Turkish Republic. There were no nostalgic memories. At least for that evening, I had moved on. Then, we walked across the street to a rooftop restaurant to have dinner under the stars. As I recall, Sevda gave a declaration that she was through with men, and I did something equally silly about women. We drank copious amounts of Jack Daniels and eventually, she poured me into a taxi that would take me back to the Eresin Crown Hotel across the Galata bridge and the Golden Horn inlet.

When I got to my room, it suddenly hit me. I was alone. For the first time in nearly 40 years, I had no wife. Officially, there was a piece of paper, but the practical part of me recognized the absolute truth. It was after midnight as I lay down on the bed without taking off my clothes. I knew I had to get some sleep because I had a meeting early the next day with the CEO of Migros, and the company's headquarters was located across the Bosporus on the Asian side. But sleep would not come.

I started fiddling with my Nokia 9500 Communicator, the computer and phone device that Tanya had given me for my 60th birthday. I absently scrolled through a list of contacts, wondering if I would do the unthinkable and call Tanya. I could use the pretense I wanted to talk to Masha or Mia, though it really wasn't a pretense. I fought the urge.

As I went through the contact list, I came upon a fairly recent addition. Her name was Olga, and she had worked for me less than six months. As I fought through the fog of drink, I recalled that I had sent her a text message a few weeks earlier when she was in Odessa handling a Nestle promotion of a jazz festival. I had asked how it was going, and then congratulated her when she said it had been very successful. At that moment, I was sitting on my balcony overlooking St. Sofia church, and wondering where on earth Tanya went on those Sunday afternoon drives she described as "her time."

I also remembered that after a few weeks on the job Olga had indicated that she was leaving our company. She had received the offer she really wanted at a rival company, Ogilvy. For some reason, perhaps just my competitive nature kicking in, I had fought hard to keep her, using tactics that were at once political and manipulative. She said she had already accepted the job, and was fearful of having to tell them she had changed her mind. "What, you mind telling the other guy, but you don't mind telling me this," I said pointedly.

I ask her to think about it overnight and then give me her answer. She did, and it was the answer for which I was looking. I remember getting up from behind my desk, and hugging her. I had never done that – with any employee.

Then, the Friday evening before the Istanbul trip and Tanya's departure, our company was handling the press for a Bryan Adams concert on Kyiv's Independence Square. In our last nearly sustained moments together, I went to the concert with Tanya and Mia. We had VIP standing room tickets not far from the stage. During the concert, I spied Olga, who was standing alone. We glanced at one another. She was dressed in a black jacket and jeans, and I thought she was the cutest girl among the half million people at the street concert. I reverted again to a text message to her – something really innocuous – but I don't think she heard it over the sound of Adams' singing "Straight from the Heart."

Lying down on my hotel room bed, propped up with a pillow, I began to feel slightly guilty thinking of this Olga in the same city as the so very recently past-tensed Tanya. Was it merely a situation of having just fallen off a bicycle? I felt slightly giddy, like a high school student whose hormones were racing like Sea Biscuit and whose acne was exploding like South Pacific volcanoes. I simply was not being myself. Myself – that rather bland and vanilla person who could run a company but whose social skills were right up there with Mr. Peepers. Even the boxer Mike Tyson, the social pugilist, occasionally did something right and interesting. I was Woody Allen, but without the Woody part and years post *Annie Hall*.

Then, I did it. I sent a blank text message to Olga's number.

I remember being rather proud of the cutesy subterfuge. The stealth strategy had left open various options, the easiest was to suggest that it had merely been sent by mistake. Why would my interest ever wander to someone so young, so unimportant to my world as I stood at the top of whatever molehill I was atop. I smiled inwardly, and then came that famously sweet sound: beep, beep. The noise startled me such that I quickly jerked up from the reclining position on the bed.

"Was this meant for me, or was it sent by mistake." The note read.

The words hung out there like stale cigarette smoke, and then engulfed me. I choked, for it contained two questions in an 11-word statement, and they begged for an answer. It was late, and I feared she might wait for sleep until I responded. At this point, one must realize I had no idea of age, marital status, or interest – especially interest. For all I knew, she could have been awakened by my faux message, and a bruiser of an annoyed husband was asking, "Who the hell is it at this hour?" These things raced gazelle-like through my mind, upsetting the crystal that had been in place for years. I was, indeed at this point, rather set in my socially conservative ways. The seconds were ticking away.

"I am sorry to disturb you. It was an accident, but obviously I was thinking about you." I gingerly typed out the words, and then quickly changed it to "I am sorry to disturb you. Yes, it was an accident. I was going through my contact list, noticed your name, and, before I knew it, had erroneously hit the send button." Then I added a sweet, "Good night."

Having sent the message, I thought about sleep. If I did not get to sleep soon, I wouldn't be worth a damn for my morning meeting, and I was satisfied with my response. Perhaps it had tickled her curiosity.

Beep, beep. That sound again. "A mistake?" The question was so stark, so direct. She was obviously reading my mind. Was she playing with me, or I with her?

I looked at my Nokia 9500 as if it were an alien being. I had started something, a missive sent into the foggy night, zipped across the Black Sea, relayed from some beam atop a hill in Odessa and ferried to the left bank sleeping district of Kyiv. But this particular person, Olga, was not sleeping.

My fingers tapped out another tentative message. "Olga, obviously I was thinking about you or I would not have landed on your name in my contact list. Best, Mike."

There were a dozen reasons I could have been thinking about her, none romantic. I was her boss, and after all she was the strategic planner for advertising in my company. I could have been pondering the Danish account we recently won. Admittedly, at half-past midnight in a Istanbul hotel, it was a rather strange fixation to which I had paid little previous attention. It was not what one would call a big dog account, certainly not up there with the tobacco company or our high-flying communications portfolio.

Beep, beep. Would she never let go of it, I remember thinking. It was not because I didn't want to hear more from her – I did. It was simply because I was afraid that another communication would bring down the reality curtain, things like age, which, though I didn't know then, separated us by three decades. However, the note was very short. "That's sweet, Mike. Good night."

It was almost as if we had an emotional connection, a cerebral meeting of the minds, if only at a certain kindergarten level. I lay my head back on the fluffy pillow and exhaled the breath that had been bottled inside me for a near eternity. I slept well. I woke up even better. The meeting on the Asian side was with a very accommodating CEO, who held out the promise that we would do a ton of business together, and eventually we did.

In the business lounge as I waited for my Turkish Airlines flight back to Kyiv, a heavy dose of reality set in. I would be coming back to an empty apartment. I was wondering if Tanya had left more than a couple of towels – the big ones, not the small ones; or, if she had stripped the bed, and where the hell had we kept the sheets. I really didn't do real life very well. I tagged along, ferried from place to place on one of those magic carpets that never seem to touch the ground.

And this new thing with Olga: Was it really a thing? While I didn't know her age, I knew she was well behind me, and when I thought about it, she was a toddler when I was flying around on Air Force Two with Sen. Byrd meeting with world leaders. She was younger than my oldest daughter by close to a decade.

It couldn't be real, or could it be. No one can ever guarantee a happy ending, though we would love to have in mind a spontaneous and gleeful conclusion, such as in the movie script for *The Graduate*, where the gauzy cinematic grand finale had a goofy Dustin Hoffman suspending disbelief at the near marriage of his true love to another fellow. I mean, do you really believe Tom Hanks stayed with Meg Ryan after that conclusive kiss at the end of *You've Got Mail*? Hell no, the guy had just robbed her of her Little Store on the Corner. If there had been one additional scene, she would have kicked him in the balls and walked away smiling.

Fast forward: It is Sept. 21, 2008, three years later, as I am writing these words. I must quickly end this chapter. Olga's daughter, Valya, whom I also call my daughter, has popped her head into the room and is calling me for breakfast on a rainy Saturday morning.

After three years of living together Olga and I were married in Charlotte, N.C. on Jan. 9, 2009. In life, there are always suspensions of disbelief.

Chapter
19

Battling the Giants

I failed to mention there was something else in my life that might have made 2005 a good year for a certain cabernet but rather toxic for the business world I inhabited. Young & Rubicam, the international agency to which we had been tethered for advertising, looked at Ukraine and got all misty at the money it felt it was losing.

It happens, and all is fair in love, war and advertising. Multiple times I saw international agencies gobble up or toss aside Kyiv-based affiliates. These are agencies that are tied to giant holding companies that live and die with the tick of the stock market. Each decision is made on how it will impact the quarterly sprint to the next earnings' report. Y&R was owned by WPP, the second-largest communications holding company in the world. WPP stood for the innocuous sounding Wire and Plastics Products. We're talking grocery market baskets turned into mega-advertising vehicles.

That they would look my way was not a surprise to me. I expected it, though not quite the tactics they used to move forward their strategy. It was stupid and clumsy. It was also underhanded, and done in the imperious manner of a company that wouldn't even consider our little enterprise a whole lunch, merely a morsel in between.

I first got a whiff of it in a telephone call from my partner for the advertising part of our business, David Payne. The call came that fateful day my wife was cleaning out our apartment and I was riding from appointment to appointment in Istanbul. It was sort of a double-whammy day.

In essence, David said he had met with Martin Beck, who oversaw Central and Eastern Europe for Y&R, and Beck indicated we would no longer be their affiliate. They wanted a wholly owned office in Kyiv, which was certainly their right. Martin had offered David some position in the Caucasus, presumably in Tbilisi, Georgia. David was smart enough to realize he was being sent into exile while at the same time being bought off. They considered me a PR guy – even though much of my life has been in advertising – and had no use for me. At that point, I had no use for them as well.

"We're going to fight them, David," I remember saying. The move by Y&R was potentially devastating to The Willard Group. They considered Philip Morris, Danone and Colgate to be network clients that would automatically switch over to the new Y&R in Kyiv. Additionally, we had several media-planning and -buying clients that would probably go into the WPP portfolio. In total, about $1 million could be sucked out of our little company quick as a cat could wink an eye, causing a loss of as much as half the workforce. Beck assumed our employees would simply and automatically become Y&R staff, at least the ones they cherry picked.

These were not clients Y&R had given us. We had fought for each one. We were there for Philip Morris in its early days in Ukraine, we won Danone in a pitch, and we wrestled Colgate away from a local agency affiliated with a non-WPP company. In other words, we had fought long and hard and had built revenues from a few thousand dollars to thousands of dollars on each account. Y&R wanted this without paying a cent. We were not going to play dead.

A year and a half earlier, WPP had purchased a large percentage in a Russian company closely tied to the Kremlin called Video International (VI). It was the VI vehicle Y&R was using to take over our business. VI had a rather checkered past during the early 90s and was rumored to have been involved in various incidents that gave rise to Russia being known as the Wild East. However, it had in recent years outgrown its earlier image. However, VI didn't do business in Eastern Europe like we did, or, in fact, we didn't believe it did business like the corporate heads in London would like to do business. This was our trump card.

There were several other factors in our favor. Young & Rubicam had been on a losing streak. A year earlier it had lost the Kraft confectionery business worldwide, which impacted our business since Kraft was one of our largest clients. However, more recently, Y&R had lost the Chesterfield account, one of Philip Morris' brands, to Leo Burnett. This meant Y&R had no international Philip Morris brands in its portfolio, and left the field wide open for Willard to challenge the advertising giant for regional brands, such as Bond Street, which we had handled for years. As for Danone, I had developed a close relationship with the managing director, Stephane Batoux, who knew we had done a good job for them over the years. Colgate, I figured, was out the door. Of the three, it was the smallest account, and primarily consisted of dubbing commercials into Ukrainian and placing media. Carefully looking at the cost-benefit, Colgate, at that time, really wasn't much of a factor in our client portfolio.

In mid-December 2005, a meeting was arranged for my brother Glen and me with Martin Beck at my Sofiyivska Street apartment. As we sat in the living room, Beck outlined Y&R's plans, which, at that point were portrayed as nebulous and simply options. We listened patiently as Beck said they were going to have a wholly owned office, but it could take several directions, including one confused scenario of an investment from an Israeli. Another was to have a company that had recently lost its Saatchi & Saatchi franchise, Adel, become the Y&R office. Video International owned Adel. The third option was to keep the status quo.

We immediately said we were for the third option, and that nothing else would do. We said we would not go quietly into the night, and that Y&R was in for a fight. I intentionally outlined our strategy – a shot over the bow – though Beck didn't appear to recognize what I was doing. It all had to do with corporate governance, the altar at which any worldwide multinational company would want to bow. I indicated to Beck that The Willard Group would not be a party to any deal with "people who don't do business like we do". My suspicion was they had already settled on the Adel/VI route, and they had.

Then, I outlined a systemic violation of what we felt were business ethics by Young & Rubicam. By the time of this meeting, they had approached two of our largest clients – Philip Morris and a mobile communications company, Astilit. Both clients had informed us of this, and were confused about what was happening. At this point, we were not only still affiliated with Y&R, we had not received a notice of termination of our affiliate agreement.

We politely asked Beck to set up a meeting in London with his superiors before he left Kyiv. He indicated he would do so, but left without setting the meeting in motion. The next day, under the contract with Y&R, we fired the initial salvo by petitioning for arbitration. This immediately got us our meeting in London with Stefan Himpe, the chief operating officer of Y&R in Europe. They also sent a notice saying they could terminate us in six months.

Both Glen, who is an attorney and a Certified Public Accountant, and I flew to London and met with Himpe, Beck and a young lawyer for Y&R. We outlined the problems we had with Y&R going behind our back to meet with Willard clients and attempting to steal away our key employees, a gambit at which they had been universally unsuccessful. They made no apologies for this but indicated that the termination notice was merely an option.

We indicated we had built our client list from scratch, and now they wanted us to turn them over without giving us a kopek in return. Himpe indicated that Y&R wasn't afraid of arbitration, and would be happy to take a dispute to the courts, either in London or Kyiv. By nature of the contract, arbitration would be in London.

The meeting was civil – but barely. We went away unsatisfied, and figuring we would be headed toward arbitration. As we delved more into this option, it appeared unrealistic in that it was on WPP and Y&R's home court and would be expensive. We had to have another plan.

During this time, I had shared my correspondence with Himpe with my public affairs contact at WPP, Fiona McEwan. A year earlier she had told me to notify her about developments that mentioned WPP or Video International. She was speaking, of course, of press reports, but I interpreted this liberally and sent her letters that questioned Y&R's commitment to corporate governance in Eastern Europe. She advised that I send them to an attorney at WPP, which I did.

I later learned through Martin Beck, via David Payne, that our campaign aimed at questioning Y&R corporate governance issues in Ukraine had an impact. They were delaying the opening of a wholly owned office for at least six months. This gave us significant running room and I started looking for a win-win result that would bring us back from the brink of confrontation.

When I heard that Y&R European President Massimo Costa was coming to Kyiv to meet with Adel, I seized the opportunity and wrote him a letter of truce, suggesting that we meet. I found him a couple of days later in the lobby of the Premier Palace Hotel, one of Kyiv's finest. We adjourned to the bar for a serious discussion.

Over a drink, I outlined a way I thought we could patch things up. I asked for a Wunderman franchise for a minimum of three years – Wunderman being the BTL agency in the Y&R family of companies

– and I asked that our affiliation with Burson-Marsteller for public relations be kept intact. Massimo was gracious but made no promises. He did, however, seem to think the Wunderman franchise could be worked out. On the B-M affiliation, he was recalcitrant, indicating that while he headed up Y&R Brands, of which B-M was part, it didn't give him authority over the public relations group. I asked him to try.

Massimo, who I instinctively liked, was good to his word, and within the next couple of days I had a letter from Himpe, the COO, with an offer of the Wunderman franchise. I felt it was a significant compromise, particularly given the fact that more and more emphasis was being placed on below-the-line activities such as promotions. With an advertising ban sure to come into effect (January 2009), Philip Morris would be engaged in even more BTL operations. I felt we had such a good relationship with Danone we would be handling its promotional activities. It seemed a win-win situation, and now all I needed was to have it in contract form.

With David Payne, I flew to London to meet with Himpe to discuss the deal more in detail. It was a pleasant meeting, and the Y&R executive said we would have a contract within the week. He also reminded me of something of which I was very aware – that we owed affiliation fees, which we had not been able to pay because Y&R had not sent signed contracts. Ukrainian law required this. I noted we had the funds, and they would be forthcoming as soon as we received the contracts.

We eventually received the signed contracts, but nothing from Y&R on a Wunderman agreement. We had already announced the affiliation in our newsletter, but it was premature. We waited. And we waited some more. It became obvious it was not coming.

About this time, Martin Beck asked for a meeting and we met for breakfast at the Premier Palace Hotel. Over coffee, he made the gross error of asking that Willard's key executives in advertising simply come over to Young & Rubicam as if they were chattel to be traded for the Wunderman franchise. I indicated to him they were all free to do as they wished, but they were good people and I didn't want to lose them. I told him he had blundered by even asking. He evidently was from a corporate culture that was oblivious to such miscues. He shrugged his shoulders and that concluded the breakfast.

Because we had not received a Wunderman contract and because of Beck's bull-in-a-china-shop actions, I felt we were being strung along. About this same time, while I was again in Istanbul, I heard from a Burson-Marsteller executive and friend, Per Heggenes, that Burson was going to buy a local Moscow and Kyiv competitor, The PBN Company, and turn it into a Burson company in those two cities. He said this was the decision of Heidi Sinclair, then the president of Europe for Burson, and he just wanted to give me the heads up on it.

We were about to be left without a Y&R or a Burson affiliation, though over the years the B-M attachment in Eastern Europe had been mainly a name, not a business generator. There were few network clients in either Ukraine or Russia. While we were to work jointly with B-M Brussels on Moscow's attempt to win the 2012 Summer Olympics – a piece of business coming through Burson – we also shared with B-M our win of the lucrative Niznhy Novgorad industrial development business.

I tried to call Heidi but couldn't get her to return my phone calls for a day. When I finally reached her, she said she had been calling me and leaving voice messages, which was interesting but untrue – at the time, I didn't have voice mail. The way she told the story, the entire idea of B-M going to PBN was that of Per Heggenes, and that she was just a bystander to the decision. I had known Heggenes for years, and I trusted him. I simply didn't believe Heidi, who left Burson a short time later and took a position with the Bill and Melinda Gates Foundation. An Englishman, Jeremy Galbraith, was named to replace her.

In the final analysis, WPP, the holding company, bought PBN, but it did not become an affiliate of Burson-Marsteller. However, after the situation with PBN, we never again bill-boarded our affiliation with the B-M affiliate network – at least in Kyiv – though we continued to have cordial relations.

The affiliate issue was not to raise its head again until nearly two years later when storm clouds again appeared quite suddenly.

Chapter
20

Up From the Crucible

In the summer of 2006, under threat from both our long-time affiliations, Y&R and Burson-Marsteller, I did something unusual for me. I took a vacation to Jordan's Dead Sea, staying at the Marriott. Between the Thai massages, mudding up in the Dead Sea, and swimming with Olga and daughter Valya, I did some serious thinking about where we were as a company, and what we needed to do.

The result was the Dead Sea Declaration, which eventually became The Willard Group Declaration of Independence. It was to become the document by which we would live, our battle cry. It was, actually, our declaration of war. For more than two years it occupied a central place in our reception area for all to see, a giant document that took up half a wall.

The Willard Group Declaration of Independence

We are invincible. We are invincible because of who we are and what we stand for. We are invincible because we dream dreams not of just growth but of fulfillment and better lives for all of the people who call The Willard Group their home.

We are invincible because, unlike international agencies, we are loyal to our people, our clients and our business partners. We believe that money should be made the old-fashioned way, by earning it.

We are convinced that no agency has ever been made better by being acquired by one of the conglomerates. In our view, these are not advertising or PR companies, they are financial companies.

They buy, sell, trade and sometimes shut down. They do not create. They do not add value. They merely morph. Sometimes they bully. We will not be bullied.

We are invincible because we report to ourselves and are accountable only to ourselves and our clients, and not stock market symbols or the whims of any gigantic holding company.

We are also invincible because we do the job we do better than the international networks to whom we have been tethered for the last decade. This is not braggadocio, merely common sense and a look at the record.

This makes us independent. We must actively assert this independence. We can no longer let huge conglomerates with homogenized ideas control our destiny. Our destiny is ours to do with what we will.

The fact is we won our clients through pitches and through hard work. Nothing was referred to us. Nothing was given to us.

We fought all the way. We built them from small clients into large clients over the last decade with no help from any international agency. All the international agency did during this period was lose business, and make it more difficult for us.

Now Y&R and WPP have chosen to come in and attempt to take those clients away from us without paying a kopek. They want a free ride on what The Willard Group has built.

They don't care about clients. They care only about 20 per cent annual growth. We care about clients, and this is why they will lose.

They attempted to shut us down. They could not. They attempted to acquire our people as if they were pawns to be traded. They could not.

We choose to be an agency of leaders and not of followers.

This will take courage and confidence. It will not always be easy, but we will always maintain our first-class service and our dedication to winning for our clients.

Agencies are about people, and their ability to do a great job. International agencies and holding companies seem not to recognize this.

The Willard Group does. This is why we will win.

We had broken the bond. The anticipation in the market was that the new Young & Rubicam, which I affectionately called Y&R Light, would clean our clock. No other affiliate in the region had stood up to its network partner. We not only suited up for battle to go toe-to-toe with the ad giant, but we had the cock-sure attitude we could actually win. Forget David and Goliath. This was the New York Yankees against the Bad News Bears.

About this time, we became pirates. Not bad pirates, but good pirates. My morning notes came with skull and crossbones at the top of the page. The Jolly Roger flew throughout the office, and we even created an ad with my assistant, Oksana Yerofeyeva with black eye-patch and sword. We woke up each morning with a single-minded attitude that we would keep our network clients longer than Y&R anticipated and develop new business. We did much better.

In the final analysis, we kept our Danone brands two years longer than Y&R thought we would, and still managed to continue to do below-the-line projects for them. In 2010 we won Danone's public relations business out-right in Ukraine. On Colgate, we won a part of the business we never previously had – promotional work. But, it was with our largest client, Philip Morris, that the real battle of Kyiv was waged. We went chin-to-chin with Young & Rubicam and won hands-down in a pitch over its popular Bond Street brand.

There was no one person responsible for this win. For the first time ever, I participated in a Philip Morris presentation as the opening speaker instead of David Payne, our director of advertising. While our entire creative group contributed in one way or another to the win, two young art directors Nikolay Yakubov and Sergey (Johnny Depp) Khandusenko led the way. I tried to set the stage for David, who would give the bulk of the presentation, backed by client leader Natasha Lotra, who gave the financial part of the pitch.

The scene was a sterile conference room with a circular table with just enough room in the middle to maneuver. I walked between openings and made my remarks directly in front of those who would be judging, walking down the line, looking into their eyes. I reminded them of our decade-long history together and that what we would show on this particular day were merely visuals and ideas. I said that this day, June 6, was merely a snapshot in time, and that we had never let them down through our long relationship. I said that the agency today before them was the same one they had always counted on for such brands as Bond Street and Chesterfield, to name two. Though it was just an eight- minute talk, I felt drained afterward. David got up and delivered a well-organized and logically constructed creative presentation. Natasha did the same on costs.

Before the evening was over, we got word that the panel felt we had a better understanding of the brand than did Y&R. The next day, this local and regional agency was told we had kept the account in competition against a mega agency. It was easily the biggest win in the history of the company.

During the fight with Y&R, I took every advantage. We could do this because we were an agency that was transparent, paid the full boat of taxes and didn't deal in the outright bribes common in our field in Eastern Europe. The profession is rife with cheats, so much so that it is systemic. Paying marketers bribes under the table for business was common practice. Even the advertising contests on many occasions were fixed. After one such so-called respectable contest, we were told that if we wanted to do better they could assure us of third place, but it would cost us. This way of doing business in Eastern Europe is so much a part of the culture that those who paid to win actually were under the delusion that they had won – or why else would they have taken first prize. It was a strange logic.

Having been a veteran consultant on many election contests at virtually every level – from a city treasurer race to U.S. Senate races – I looked on our fight with Young & Rubicam not so much as a corporate battle but as I would a political race, one in which we were the underdog. We had to fight a gritty, focused and, in some cases, outrageous campaign. Hence, the Dead Sea Declaration that became Willard's Declaration of Independence, as well as our transformation into pirates.

Additionally, I put our community marketing website, *PRschik*.com, to good use. I was interviewed on several occasions in a question and answer format. This gave me an opportunity to get our message out unfettered and uncluttered, and then have our team hang releases on the comments in the trade press.

During this time, I also raised our profile by taking on the relatively new CEO of Burson-Marsteller, Mark Penn, and the CEO of WPP, the much-heralded Martin Sorrell. In the first instance, it was something I would have been happier not to have done.

Penn made the tragic mistake of sacrificing B-M's non-partisan image by illogically taking on the Hillary Clinton for President campaign, while Sorrell pursued a couple of rascals in court he accused of slandering him – thereby causing even more attention to a non-issue in which he won a Pyrrhic victory while losing the PR war. Both were studies in what not to do as CEOs of respected companies.

In Penn's case, B-M had always stayed out of political contests.

In an organization with more than 2,000 professional staffers, a company has multiple political persuasions. I could picture "Burson Staffers for Barack Obama" committees being formed. Also, as the saying goes, what goes around comes around. Certainly, B-M's clients – such as Philip Morris – had to cringe when Penn made the announcement the company would, in essence, back Sen. Clinton. By being a high-profile advocate of a political candidate, it opened other areas of the business to conflicts of interests.

It was in January 2007, while attending the Davos World Economic Forum in Switzerland, Penn put on his blog that B-M would take Sen. Clinton onboard as a client. He had previously been an advisor and pollster for President Bill Clinton. Several Burson employees wrote back to the blog in true suck-up fashion that they were happy the 50-plus year-old company had become involved in a partisan political fight for the first time. However, these were the younger, less-experienced professionals. Those that had been around for some time were bewildered, groaned or just shook their heads.

That night, I wrote back to Penn's blog that it was a mistake to take on a partisan contest and that it would haunt Burson-Marsteller in the future. I noted that while Willard had often been asked to handle Ukrainian political candidates, we had always stood by Burson's credo and refused to do so. Penn immediately wrote back that he, that very night, was having dinner with a firm that had worked in Ukrainian politics and had been very successful with commercial businesses. He didn't mention the name, but he was referring to Paul Manafort of Davis, Manafort & Freedman, a firm that had been tangentially involved in the comeback of the nation's Regions Party and its head, Viktor Yanukovich.

What Penn did not write, however, was that Manafort's company did not do extensive commercial business in Ukraine, or that giving Manafort credit for winning for the Regions Party stretched credulity to the stratosphere. Western influence on Ukrainian races is often exaggerated, as was the case when several consultants in the United States claimed credit for Boris Yeltsin's win in Russia in the mid-1990s. In neither case did the Ukrainian nor the Russian politicians give credit to American firms for the victory.

Penn should have stepped down from his role as CEO of Burson-Marsteller, something most B-M executives with whom I have talked now agree. A leave of absence would have been expected and understood, given Penn's closeness at that time to the Clintons.

Postscript: In the midst of the Democratic presidential primary fight between Clinton and Obama, there were several disclosures that pointed to the illogic of B-M being involved in the race to such a degree. In the first instance, a Penn client, Blackwater, a company providing private security in Iraq, was accused of using poor judgment when civilians died during shootouts. It was front-page news and the subject of a Congressional inquiry. Then later, it came out that Penn had attended a meeting with Colombian government officials – the government was a client of B-M's – on an issue that Sen. Clinton had issued statements opposing. Penn became a target, arguably an unfair one, when Obama pulled ahead in the delegate count. The charge was that Penn had taken a sure winner and made her a loser. When the professional reputation of a CEO is tarnished, some of the glow comes off the company as well.

As for Sir Martin, his pursuing in court the settling of a personal grievance did less to harm WPP's image, but it did hold him up to ridicule, at least for a while.

What raised the ire of – if not Martin Sorrel, then those around him – was a column I wrote which appeared in O'Dwyer's PR News, an international publication on public relations. I'll let the column tell the story:

In the beginning, I said let Sir Martin Sorrell be Sir Martin. After all, the colorful WPP chief was merely attempting to make a high-profile statement about the careless use of anonymous junkyard blogs that he felt defamed him. But that was before the libel trial he instigated ended in, at best, a Pyrrhic victory, about as satisfying as kissing your sister (a southern expression generally used long ago when American football games ended in a frustrating tie).

Sir Martin won the court case, sort of. He agreed to the same amount of money he would have received if the trial had not gone on two weeks, about $238,000, in a suit that cost him and WPP about $2 million. Not a good business trade-off. Still, Sorrell declared victory. The defendants, two Italian former employees, accused Sir Martin of abandoning the battlefield before they had a chance to present their case. The defendants never admitted guilt.

Everyone in the ad and PR world probably knew the story by now as it dragged on. Sir Martin took the former employees to court for allegedly libeling him on an anonymous blog, saying he was Mafioso, a money launderer and calling him a "mad dwarf". As blogs go – in a world of rather silly literary meanderings – this one apparently was more juvenile than most. Sir Martin is certainly no gangster, and being vertically challenged is no big deal. A lot of us are.

Sorrell, however, felt the blogs somehow hurt his reputation and that of WPP. There was also a woman involved, but that, while titillating and appealing to prurient interests, really isn't relevant to this narrative. That is to say: A court of law is rarely the place – at least it should be a last resort – to seek redress when one feels a reputation has been damaged.

Obviously, Sorrell felt the offense was major, and so suited up for battle. He said he could not "think of a more comprehensive attack" on his character. The blog entries, including an embarrassing image, were sent to executives of rival ad companies. It is doubtful, however, that the offending blogs were more than white noise filtering through the backwaters of our communications industry, not something that would cause even a slight quiver of the WPP empire, much less a seismic reaction. The stock continued to march upward. Sorrell's legal action, though, revved the sounds of silence of this relatively minor happening into a story heard far and wide, as if blasted through the speakers at a Rolling Stones' concert. In fact, the words "mad dwarf + Martin" turns up more than a half million Google references, which is a half million more than if the case had been kept in Sir Martin's pocket.

There are strange ironies here: There is no corporation on earth that has more public relations talent in its stable than does WPP, which includes, among others, the PR giants Burson-Marsteller, founded by the still active Harold Burson and Hill & Knowlton. Why didn't he turn to them?

Virtually any senior public relations counselor would have suggested to Sir Martin that the blogs were: 1) Not mainstream press and had limited shelf life; 2) That they appeared the work of infantile, grudge-driven people; and 3) Most importantly, that the most reputation-damaging verbiage was not in the least believable. In other words, the affront – regardless of intent – would not materially impact WPP's balance sheet or, in the final analysis, Martin Sorrell's reputation. It was a merely a snapshot moment of trash talk.

Having decided to go to trial, however, one assumed Sir Martin had a higher calling – a substantive point to make about the individual needing some protection in a wacky, blogosphere world where anything goes. He didn't. The hurricane that was Sir Martin's outrage and wrath came ashore, turning nary a leaf, much less taking roofs off houses.

The next time Sir Martin decides to spend millions on a suit, he might pause and reflect, and then reach for the telephone number of Harold Burson.

I personally don't think Sir Martin even noticed the column. He's got an empire to run. However, the people around him did and this filtered over to Burson-Marsteller. It was brought up with me in one of the various discussions with B-M executives. But by the time it was, we had already declared victory. We had not only managed to stay in business, but had set back Y&R's plans in Ukraine, giving us time to regroup and rethink our business. In the meantime, we kept our largest account, Philip Morris, and began picking up others.

Gloating, however, does not become anyone, particularly us in this business. Most battles are merely skirmishes for larger things to come. We realized that we are only as good as tomorrow's ad or public relations campaign. In this game, which is very subjective, you can be king of the hill one day and the next day suggesting to a client you will walk his dogs if he will only sign on the dotted line.

And this is what happened to Willard.

Chapter
21

Making the Tough Decisions

A not-so-funny thing happened on the way to our becoming a resounding success in Eastern Europe: Our wheels came off and we veered toward a ditch. It happened quite suddenly. Perhaps we were feeling a little too confident.

We had done a good job of fighting off challenges from WPP and Young & Rubicam, but it had been costly. We had beefed up staff, increased pay for most all, and paid out virtually our yearly profits in staff bonuses to make sure we kept the best professional staff around. It was a defensive action on the chessboard, and we were playing hardball. Mentally, I figured how long we could run losing about $50,000 a month before we had a cash crunch. I put it at six, though, on paper, it could be a few months longer.

Y&R had made a run at our two top executives in advertising, Natasha Lotra who ran our Philip Morris business and Tania Spiridonova, who at that time served as client services director. Both were with me back in 1994 when I headed up the government-funded education program. I didn't want to lose them, and knew if we did it would be a crippling blow at the worst time. From the standpoint of morale, it would be devastating to see long-time employees defecting to the other side.

Lotra met with Y&R and simply told them "no thanks." She

answers to a different drummer, and I felt confident she would stay in the fold. Spiridonova, however, was offered the job of CEO of the new Y&R Ukraine and it was tempting. For at least 24 hours, she took the position. When I heard, I was crestfallen, and expressed this to her. Y&R wasn't a competitor. It was the enemy. Both women were at a time in their lives where they were reexamining priorities, wondering what such a long time at Willard actually meant.

While I owned the company, with a small percentage to my brother, Glen, I was in a three-way partnership. However, Glen long ago had taken a backseat, realizing he really didn't want to be involved in the day-to-day operations. In essence, he turned over his interest in the partnership to me. David Payne had one-third. Glen continued to be valuable as both a legal and financial consultant. However, at this point, there wasn't room for partners who took a lot of money out of the coffers.

For better or worse, a long-time rap for or against me was that I tended to initiate and execute 95 per cent of the decisions in the company. I believe in team play and input, but I believe that a business is not a democracy but a benevolent dictatorship. Otherwise, decisions take forever, and decision by committee is slow death when it comes to crucial issues. This is particular true with a relatively small business operating in risky markets. My closest advisor on crisis issues was Glen, and we generally were on the same wavelength, but not always.

Making David a partner was something that was not necessary way back in 1998 when we were closing a deal with Burson-Marsteller and Y&R, but I did it anyway. In attitude and culture, David was always more of an employee. This is to take nothing away from David as a strategic advertising guy. He was good at what he did and made a valuable contribution to the business.

Tania Spiridonova stayed away from work that day to think

about the job offer she had taken, and I believe it weighed heavily on her that some might consider she was betraying her long-time friends and colleagues. Additionally, Roman Diukarev flew down and had a heart-to heart discussion with her. They had been friends for many years, and Roman had originally hired her for, ironically, an early Moscow Y&R project in Ukraine. Roman himself had been a PR guy with the advertising agency, but that had been long ago. Toward mid-afternoon, Tania called me and asked if she and her husband could have dinner with Olga and me. We met at a Kyiv steakhouse, Soho.

That evening, I felt like I was fighting for more than just to retain a good employee and person. I felt like I was fighting for the heart and soul of the agency. As we sat down with Tania and her husband, Victor, I had only one thing on my mind – keeping her at Willard. Otherwise, I felt the dam could burst. I reminded her of our years together, and told her that we could not part as friends if she were to land at Y&R. She was hugely conflicted, but in the end reached across the table, grabbed my hand, and said she was staying at Willard. I was relieved, but most of all I was proud of Tania for making what I felt then and now was the right decision for her.

But I also put a monetary incentive on the table, and the next day called in Natasha and Tania separately. After consulting with David, I named Tania president of advertising and boosted both Tania and Natasha's salaries by a considerable amount, probably the highest in the market at the time. Time, I believe, has proven it to be a good decision, particularly in light of subsequent events. Other than David, Tania was already the senior person in advertising, and Natasha was legend in her stewardship of the Philip Morris account.

Most of the turmoil occurred in the spring and summer of 2007. Earlier that year, we had picked up advertising work with Ramstore, a chain that operated hypermarkets throughout Russia. Previously, we had just been engaged for public relations in Moscow. However, I had met often with the parent company Migros in Istanbul, and we were well-known to its senior management. This, I believe, helped get us the invitation to pitch the advertising business. Ordinarily, it is difficult for a company from Ukraine to win Moscow advertising business, but we broke the barrier. David did a good job of presenting a strategy to them that focused on image and service and not on the standard grocery store marketing on price. We were feeling very confident and took on two very expensive creatives from Moscow to work in Russia and Ukraine.

At this same time, we won an advertising assignment from a Ukrainian vodka company that we thought would be a large client. It wasn't. Late in 2007, Ramstore advertising went away when it was put up for sale. Then, our closest contact with the Soyuz Victan vodka company, the CEO, left his position.

With a rise in inflation, the economy began to slow down. Danone, our third-largest advertising client, reduced its spending with us to almost nothing. Because of inflation, they were having a harder time moving their products, and took more work in-house.

The situation in Moscow was also changing. The office had done extraordinarily well, but had devoted so many resources to an industrial development project for the city of Nizhny Novgorod, it had not the opportunity to followed up on new business leads. When the Nizhny Novgorod project concluded, we fell into the red zone when it came to profitability. To use a rather trite term, we were heading face forward into the so-called perfect storm.

In April 2008, we had our first real loss. I began looking down the road, and I could not see sufficient work in the pipeline. Taking a telescopic gander at May and June, I could see sizable losses. I called the executive team together, and gave them the unvarnished picture. The good news was that we didn't owe anyone. We had no loans and were current with our vendors. In some cases, we had even pre-paid on behalf of our our clients. We had a fairly substantial amount of cash in one of several banks in Kyiv, Moscow and abroad. Unlike many firms, we had invested back into Willard over the years. We could take a hit to the solar plexus and end up with only a tummy ache, painful but not fatal. At the meeting, I unveiled a plan for a turn-around. One aspect was reduction of management costs. The timetable I set for return to profitability was not until September. It was then the beginning of May.

When it came right down to it, we had never been wasteful. We could cut operational expenses – not staff – slightly but we had already addressed and clamped down on communication and transportation expenses. I saw only three areas to reduce expenses, and I felt none would severely impact the business, but they would be painful.

In mid-May, Glen and I met with David. Before he was called into the meeting, I believe David knew what was happening. His activity in the company had diminished over the years, particularly as a strong Ukrainian staff took on more and more duties in advertising. David had often remarked to me that he was not as useful to the company in its current format. He was right. I informed him as gently as I could that I was dissolving the partnership

Any partnership that lasts 10 years has to be considered a success. During that time, David and I had numerous disagreements, but generally not on matters of substance, generally about style. He was a 9-to-6 employee, while I often came in before 7 a.m. and rarely wrapped up before 8 p.m. His approach was probably the sanest, but mine dealt with the realities of operating a small company in extremely risky markets.

Overall, David and I had a good partnership, but one we both probably felt was one-sided. From his side, he felt I pulled all the levers, and he felt marginalized. Generally, what I said became gospel. I believe in soliciting opinions, but in the end making decisions as a CEO and not a collective. From my side, I had worked in a partnership once before – and from a working standpoint that partnership went very well. In it, we both worked as employers and not employees, and therefore it was easier for us to come together both on style and substance. I fell I lacked this with David. If I really needed help in making a decision, I turned to my brother, Glen, who I felt best embodied the entrepreneurial spirit that was inside of me. If not Glen, I bounced ideas off Roman Diukarev in Moscow. Later, a close advisor would be my wife, Olga.

In the end, David landed on his feet, securing a job at a Kyiv-based marketing company, Pulse, where, due to the larger collection of expats, I felt he was more comfortable.

Though I actually saw it coming at least a year earlier, dissolving the partnership was a tough decision. It would not have come if it had not been forced by what I felt could become a precarious economic situation.

The second decision was much easier. I flew to Moscow and fired the two expensive creatives I had hired six months earlier. I had been told they could "take us to a different level". I should have asked the question whether that level was up or down. In my view, they were not as advertised and the proof was in the creative product, which became slightly more cutesy but not, in my view, as rational for consumers. It was a man and wife team – an art director and a creative director – both very nice people, but, as a team, they were not quite ready for the roles they assumed, even if they did come from the larger and supposedly more sophisticated market of Moscow. The husband art director was very capable and experienced, and if they had not come as a team he would have been a sure keeper. However, they committed a sin worse than not being at the top of the game. They didn't seem to want to be involved in the nitty-gritty of the game. They were dogmatic in their approach to their own creative ideas, which can be admirable, but not to the point of obstinacy. They had been warned that I was in Moscow to let them go, and they drove a hard bargain, threatening legal action. I kept them on a month longer than I intended, and I wasn't happy about it.

Finally, I made the decision to move our offices from downtown Kyiv to what I now refer to as the "fashionable" Left Bank of the Dnipro River. It was a move I would like to think we would have made anyway. We cut our rent by substantially more than a third, and, in the end, had more interesting space for an ad and PR agency.

A couple of months earlier, I sent out a Willard Notes in which I envisioned the office of my dreams. It began:

"Hold on to the side of your desks...

Picture an office – not really an office but a clubhouse – at the very end of some Kyiv metro route. Picture that office as not having individual offices, but perhaps a handful of work stations. Picture several conference rooms, one large, one smaller, with great presentation equipment. Picture in that office our financial and legal. Picture, perhaps, other administration facilities, but a minimal amount. Picture a nice, relaxing area for employees and clients when, and if, they visit.

Picture an office where the CEO has no office, but can use one of the workstations. Picture an office where everyone has – no desk, no specific computer, but – yep, his or her own personal drawer. Picture art directors, client leaders, client executives on both the ad and PR side armed with state-of-the-art laptops working from anywhere and everywhere – the local coffee house with Wi-Fi, home, a park. Picture meetings by video Skype.

Let's take it a step further. Picture a once a month gathering of all employees, in the summer in a park, or in the winter at a suitable restaurant. Picture a situation where employees rarely go to the clubhouse, except for certain needs.

Picture the name on the clubhouse being Willard. Imagine the responsibility. Then, imagine the freedom.

Anyone who has any thoughts on the above, please send me a note. We are in an electronically nomadic world. We should adapt to it for efficiency, and our own social fulfillment."

We never achieved this ideal, but we came pretty close. It wasn't a handful of workstations, but a sufficient number to seat all our employees. It wasn't the last Metro stop, either, but one just across the river on what was called the Left Bank. At one time, it had been a dacha area, but as people pushed the boundaries of Kyiv proper, it became what Ukrainians call "sleeping areas" with huge, high-rise apartment buildings reaching to the sky. However, we were a stone's toss from the river, and there were modern houses intermixed with less expensive dacha houses. In other words, it was country without being country. You could hear a rooster crow in the morning but we were two minutes from one of the busiest thoroughfares just outside Kyiv

The building was constructed as a modern house, but inside was made to house a small company. It was less space than we had previously, but more interesting space. We did away with desks, except for one in my office that also served as a second conference room, and just had workstations. I encouraged our staff to use a different workstation each day. "Move around," I said. "Get to know one another better." It took a while to catch on, since most employees were used to their own desk and immediately took up nesting at a certain spot.

The first two weeks after we moved in, it rained almost every day. But when it stopped, I was happy to see people utilizing their wireless laptops in the courtyard, sitting underneath sun umbrellas and at tables and chairs we had put in the courtyard. We were about a five-minute walk from the nearest subway. Additionally, I encouraged people to work from home, or a café, or anywhere. The most important thing was that we do good work and we meet deadlines.

There was some question among our professional staff that moving the office from downtown Kyiv might be seen as a retrenchment – that we were doing poorly. I put it another way: "When I meet with the head of Philip Morris or Danone and tell them we moved across the river and saved nearly $200,000 a year in rent and have better offices, they will say it was a smart move. No, they will say brilliant."

This was the time of the global market letdown at the tail end of summer, 2008. "AIG, Goldman Sachs, Merrill Lynch, Fannie Mae and Fannie Mac – they have problems. We have issues. We have solved our problems," I told them.

We had, indeed, we had trimmed about $800,000 from our yearly expenses, and we had achieved this in three months without, in my view, impairing our service. By August we were back in the profit column, one month earlier than my prognosis. When I look back on it, it was an amazing accomplishment, but it was a difficult, even painful one.

In the meantime, we had been successful in winning back a chunk of some old business and some new business. As we headed into the winter, all was right with the world. For now.

Postscript: As I put the finishing touches on this book in May 2010, the world seems to be slowly emerging from a deep recession. Because of decisions made in the summer of 2008, we as a company managed to eke out a small profit throughout the recession. Our public relations business actually grew and we held our own in the advertising arena.

I also made a few personal decisions. It was time I stepped away from the day-to-day operation of the agency and looked at the larger picture. I dropped the title CEO, and kept only chairman, though often referring to myself as the Chief Imagination Officer. We were in our 12th year and it was time for someone else to take charge of the Kyiv office. In Moscow, I had long since decided that Roman Diukarev was the person to make virtually all the decisions there. He conferred with me, but I don't remember a time not agreeing with him.

In Kyiv, I looked to what I felt would be the logical choice, Olga

Willard. Willard is a family business and as I looked to the future I wanted someone I knew was not only capable but also shared my vision. She had served on the executive team for two years, and was the agency's strategic planner. She had more agency experience by virtue of working for multiple agencies in Ukraine. There were certainly other capable people, particularly Tania Spiridonova, head of advertising, and Natasha Lotra, client leader for Philip Morris. Either could have taken over the Kyiv office, but their vision might not reflect the slightly weird Willard vision.

My intention was to concentrate more on the magazine we launched in August 2009, Willard Marketing Monthly, to offer senior counsel and training to clients, to develop new business and to write books. Also, I wanted to spend a little more time with my paint brushes and oils. This was the harbor I sought, though I confess it has been difficult to find time for the painting and the writing. Maybe it will come.

Chapter
22

Where Are We Headed?

I think I would be derelict in my duty not to venture into the wild yonder when it comes to giving a broad-brush view as to where I think my twin disciplines of advertising and public relations are headed.

While the civilians who wandered onto these pages by happenstance and stayed for the journey might skip this portion, I suggest you stay with me. I promise you will learn something that could be useful in your business.

The fact is, these are two professions that, in one-way or another, touch all – from lawyer and doctor to preacher man.

Everything you do is interesting to somebody or something, even if it's just a trip to the market to pick up Alpo for the pooch. The pooch would be sorely disappointed if you came home empty handed. Extend this theory to the husband, wife, girlfriend or boyfriend. Every act, miniscule or major, influences some audience. We all deal with our individual publics and with larger publics. At some point, this becomes a word I love to hate, public relations.

Though I have told this story many times before college students, the use of public relations is biblical.

"God, listen," says Adam. His voice was strong, unwavering. He was a good spokesperson. "Yes, we ate the apple. It was a mistake. We have taken action to make sure it will not happen again. To make up for our mistake, we are planting a million new apple trees, mostly Golden Delicious."

God wasn't buying it. She was still angry.

This was a long time ago, eons prior to perception management or Big Think philosophy as defined by the so-called founder of public relations, Edward Berneys. Perhaps Adam should have left the talking to Eve, or maybe added with gusto, "Oh, and we fired the ugly serpent that caused all this mess in the first place."

In its more concrete form, apart from the rhetorical reference above, advertising pre-dates the official profession of public relations, and both are, I would argue, true professions. This is not to say that merely professionals engage in the two disciplines. There are container ship loads of charlatans who call themselves PR specialists and advertising gurus. One rarely needs more than a hammer, nail, board, paint and a piece of string to tack a sign on the office door reading PR or advertising. In most cases, there are no exacting legal standards – nor should there be – or do they have more than an informal code of conduct.

The fact that I can say public relations and advertising in the same breath I realize is heresy to those that argue that they are such separate disciplines a common mention is incongruous at best. Never a guy to give a Sherman-esque answer to a Solomon-esque question, I tend to equivocate when the query is posted comparing the effectiveness of advertising and public relations.

But since I am chairman of an advertising and public relations company, it is a question I receive with regularity – sort of like asking a chef whether he favors the preparation of sauces or soups. There are purists who suggest one cannot serve the two masters. They say one can't walk, chew gum and twang Hank Williams songs at the same time, and it is the same with practicing both advertising and public relations.

They are wrong.

I can do the Hank Williams thing, though perhaps out of tune. And I equally love the fields of advertising and public relations if for no other reason than they have kept my family fed for more than three decades. But, there are other reasons.

For starters, I am in PR for the same reason I am in advertising – both require an element of creativity, the exercise of which I find exhilarating whether it has to do with writing a PR communications strategy or crafting an ad.

If one isn't in public relations for the creative challenge, I question that person's reason for being in PR. It goes without saying that if one would prefer to be an account order taker, working at McJones Hamburger Emporium could have the same thrill.

In fact, and this will really send PR professors up a wall and ad executives yelling fakir, I think the two professions should be more closely entwined. Both the PR and the ad folks should be in the same cockpit when a new brand takes off, a critical issue addressed or a marketing plan developed.

Often, though, they are not in the same town, or, it seems, on the same planet.

To take this one step further – and written with the righteous certitude and self-interest of one who is immersed in both disciplines – it does no harm if the same company delivers both creative services. Having undressed my conflicts, I will try to convince a skeptical audience.

Many combined PR and advertising companies come about for economic reasons in small markets. The first public relations company I launched quickly became an advertising company as well when the first client to walk through the door needed a radio script written and produced. It was for a locally owned Holiday Inn's Mesquite Grill in Charleston, West Virginia. I hung out a second shingle.

Currently, my company, headquartered in Kyiv, Ukraine, is about to launch a technological product. We have worked with the client for two years, and even suggested the product. In other words, we have become passionate about its success. At this point, I don't want an interloper joining the mix.

This has nothing to do with wanting to capture all possible revenue – which, by the way, is an admirable objective – but everything to do with not wanting Ad Agency X playing Beethoven while PR Agency Y is playing Brahms.

Whether it is advertising or public relations, the name of the game is the creditable and creative delivery of messages. When it comes down to it, this is the shared DNA of everything we do. If we had a Holy Grail, this would be it.

Too many times, I have seen advertising executives and creatives at loggerheads with PR types over a creative approach to an account because both lacked the basic understanding of each other's reason for being – what the chain gang captain in Cool Hand Luke called "a failure to communicate."

It certainly didn't help with the release of a rather shallow book called "The Fall of Advertising and the Rise of PR" a few years ago. The book gave PR – previously marginalized by the ad world – phony reasons to chest beat and shout hallelujah.

More properly, the book should have preached the rise of advertising and the rise of PR. Both professions are in flux and dramatic change, primarily due to the Internet and the emergence of social media, but neither is on the decline.

When separate ad and PR companies tackle a marketing project, it is often not dynamic tension – which can be good – but negative tension. It often results in confused messages and fundamental disagreements about the delivery of those messages.

Often, even if they are from the same giant holding company

– which is the rule these days – they meet around the client table almost more as competitors than colleagues. Then, they go off and lampoon one another. In such cases, the ad folks are on Venus while the PR folks are on Mars, or vice versa. Being from the same company, sharing the same creative values, and passionately believing in the same messages and how to deliver them, bring both the ad and the PR people a little closer to earth.

But there are other factors at play. PR has come a long way from press agentry, where the primary job was to get media attention, and advertising has come just as far from those silly television jingles and dancing monkeys. The competition for the consumers' attention is fierce. The 10-year-old who once watched television's Romper Room now only has eyes for the latest computer game. It is a cliché to say that the Internet has changed everything having to do with what messages we receive and how we receive them. That happened oh so long ago.

Also, the audience is more diversified, as are the number of television options. At one time, public television fit neatly into a void with educational specials, cultural entertainment and how-to programming. Today, though it still exists, the need for public television has been greatly diminished. No, it is simply not needed, what with many homes getting a 100-plus range of channel options that serve up more than any consumer could hope for or have time to watch.

The challenge, of course, is how to reach that stratified audience. It certainly is not to toss messages into consumer-land and hope they stick. In today's world, the advertiser or the PR marketer has to tap the consumer on the shoulder, turn him around, and metaphorically shake his hand. No, better yet, give him a hug.

This doesn't call for traditional advertising or traditional public relations. It does call for a married and genetically modified version of both. It calls for a personal brand of communication that moves to action rather than annoys or even entertains. At the same time, this communication must have as its common denominator honesty and transparency. It can't be about forming phony front organizations or enlisting viral communication so fictionally scripted as to have as its main objective the fooling of the consumer. These techniques, never good, have already contaminated the chow mix of new communications techniques. In fact, given a fairly smart public, they had the life of sand flowing through a three-minute egg timer.

So, how do you reach the consumer in the 21st century?

First, shred yourself of that which worked well up until the 1990s, even beyond in some countries, those little 30- or even 60-second movies that advertising agencies so like to make and show off at award ceremonies. You will have to convince the global marketer of Colgate, P&G, Kraft and a host of others that the battle is not over gross rating points but over hearts and minds. That which floats loftily above rarely makes a personal connection. This seems as obvious as rainwater, but for some reason there seems a conspiracy to stick with the tried and true.

Secondly, think locally. The late Speaker of the U.S. House of Representatives, Tip O'Neill, said that all politics are local. He should have moonlighted as a futuristic ad or PR guy. But don't think in terms of segmented groups such as "soccer moms", or "teenagers with acne", but more in terms of attitudes and emotional buttons. In other words, moms who would do anything for their children and teenagers whose greatest fear is being considered unattractive. These are messages not easily lassoed under narrower segments but they are sufficiently localized to deliver specific messages to specific audiences.

Thirdly, throw out the old axiom that there is nothing new under the sun. There is, or else inventors wouldn't invent and talented writers wouldn't keep coming up with television programming that is actually getting better by the year. Toss off that yoke. Clear your mind. And do a little of what I call Galaxy Thinking,

In my version of Galaxy Thinking, it is concepting the weirdly possible but improbable, that which can cut through the clutter because it is purposefully unconventional. This takes a mind devoid of social and political hang-ups, and one that is able to grab on to an extraordinary idea because it is being conceived in another dimension, a near-parallel world. In the larger sense, we are talking about thinking that led to the Internet as it is today; Col. Harlan Sanders building a fried chicken empire after he became a pensioner or Ted Turner turning a small Atlanta TV station into a global communications platform. They all began with an idea that at first blush appeared impossible.

We need to apply the same Galaxy Thinking process to the ways in which we communicate benefits for and market goods and services. It is merely a way of thinking, and not really a revolutionary one. It does, however, require a winnowing of prejudices and an mind as open as a Kansas prairie.

I have, for the moment, departed somewhat from the chronological account of Willard, the company. Hopefully, I have not steered you up a dark alley and you are still with me as we head to the "final" chapter.

Chapter
23

The Optimistic Alien: The Next (Not Last) Chapter

It is difficult to wrap up what is, in essence, a memoir of a small business in a risky market. It is as if to say that the story ends here. It doesn't – not nearly. When I turned 50, I put the pedal to the metal and picked up speed. If I slowed down any at 60, I don't think anyone noticed. At mile-marker 65, one can only hope that health remains good, the political climate relatively stable for a difficult market, and my personal life as serene as it is now.

Serene is probably not the right word. It has the ring of complacency. After years of being clueless, Olga has taught me that you have to put more effort into such things as marriage if you want them to survive. This seems obvious these days to the 50 per cent of people who stay married to the same person.

You can't have three wives and five children (adopted or otherwise) with them – and ranging in age from nine to 40 plus – and hope to travel lightly. Responsibilities are heavy. That's why they are called responsibilities and come with the territory of having a more diversified – maybe even more interesting – life than the next fellow.

But I have been fortunate. The three best things that ever happened to me appeared as tragedies at the time: A possible bankruptcy, a second divorce and a brush-by acquaintance with being fired. In one way or another, I have described each in this book.

The economic conditions in West Virginia led me to start a new career in international public relations at age 50. It was a good move because the decision ferried me to Ukraine and a new life. The second divorce numbed me to the bone, but without it, I would not have met and fallen in love with Olga who has been an inspiration to me. Finally, if I had not lost out in a power struggle for leadership in Moscow in 1998, it would not have led me back to Kyiv, a renewed entrepreneurial spirit and the founding of Willard.

In each case, I could not peer into the future. I was guided by survival instincts that led me to make the right next move. There was never a roadmap, a grand strategy, merely putting one foot in front of the next and pushing forward with certain optimism.

Do I have regrets? Yes. I would be soulless if I didn't. I can say that most everything that happened to me was a recoverable happening, and every misery I might have caused had, I hope, short-term impact. I have always been cognizant of people's feelings, often times internalizing them to the extreme.

As to living and working in an emerging market (emerging sounds better than risky), it is not for everyone. In fact, it is not for even most everyone. It is for a few. It is interesting that the longer I live in Eastern Europe, the cultural differences do not merge like whitecaps and blue water but tend to be even more pronounced. Having endured and prevailed, though, one takes such things in stride. Patience is a universal virtue, but one should wear it like a favorite old sweater in Eastern Europe.

At last count, in 16 years, I had seen 12 prime ministers, and three presidents in Ukraine. Looking toward that other home, the U.S., most of my aunts and uncles died over this period. I slipped quickly from 49 to 65, and I had both a daughter and a son get married and produce five grandchildren between them. I was able to attend my son's wedding, but missed my daughter's. I console myself that it was only her official marriage. She had been married to Ken in a Las Vegas chapel wedding, complete with an Elvis impersonator crooning what Elvis impersonators croon.

There are those who say, as I outlined in the first chapter, that we who have landed in Eastern Europe as expatriates – and I despise the word for it smacks of anti-patriotism which it is not – are the types of folks who couldn't make it elsewhere. For some reason, a few Ukrainians make this argument, as if why would anyone come and settle in a land so far away from the nest and one that can be, if you let it, brutal in the business arena. On the contrary, I have found most entrepreneurial business people – whether American, British, French, German or otherwise – to be tough, smart and resourceful.

There are those, of course, primarily working for government organizations, who see Ukraine as a 15-minute layover before their next post. Additionally, there are those who work for giant multi-national companies who are three years and out. However, it takes the same attributes to make it as a country manager of a large corporation in a risky market as it does the entrepreneurial businessperson who set up shop for a lifetime. Both carry the burden of risk, as if toting a backpack of solid granite.

I am often asked my advice to companies that would like to set up shop in Ukraine. As I said in a short speech recently to a Virginia industrial development group: "Come on in. The water's fine. But watch out for a few jellyfish."

The fact is that Ukraine is a nation of 47 million consumers that smoke Marlboros, clean their bathrooms, drink Coca-Cola and like the latest electronic gadget. It has a growing middle class. "If you have a better mousetrap, a tastier cola or a gee-whiz electronic thingamabob, then this is the place for you."

I then went on to list my **Five Rules for Success in Risky Markets:**

1) Avoid coyote ugly. You know, when you wake up in the morning after a wild night, and you would rather gnaw off your arm than disturb the person next to you. This is rather trite terminology, but it fits. Jumping in bed with the wrong local business partner is the No. 1 miscalculation. It is so important because it is so costly. Often, it kills the business; or, at least, your involvement in that business. This has been the case with mega oil companies and top 10 mobile phone companies as well as the small bar on the corner.

Due diligence is a must. Never make decisions on local partners by long distance. Never rely solely on a word of mouth recommendation. Never take credentials for granted. They are often inflated.

2) Don't be a nattering nabob of negativism, to quote a line the late William Safire wrote for a failed vice president. Be practical, but be positive. The alternative simply is not productive. We advise clients to take a positive but realistic attitude. Constantly haranguing the government – even if it deserves it – is to join the doomsday chorus. A positive approach will open many more doors, whether with local business opportunities or with the government. This is one of those syrupy bromides, but it works.

3) Watch out for barstool philosophers. Opinions are like, well, bald spots, most of us eventually have one. When the economic crisis of 1998 hit, it seemed everyone at the local waterhole had an opinion on the ruble and the hryvnia. Most overstated the case. Being alarmist draws a larger crowd. Beyond this, however, are the grizzled cowboys who operate just a shade outside the law, both of their own country and that of the host country. Listen to them. It's entertaining. Don't take their advice.

4) Practice the Theory of Diminished Expectations. This won't win you any points with the folks in the boardroom back home, but it will keep you from becoming a basket case. Too often companies expect from governments and people in Eastern Europe what they couldn't hope to accomplish in their own countries. They rationalize this by saying the risks are greater. Be patient.

5) Avoid flying under the radar. You can't and won't go unnoticed. If you employ people and sell a product, you're on everyone's scope from the local gangsters to government officials, which might be one and the same.

Don't be ostentatious, but do be strategic in your awareness program. Good corporation citizenship creates a reservoir of good will. Strategic outreach programs with government officials as well as media opportunities can help avoid pitfalls later.

In summary, there is no holy writ. Surviving and thriving in Eastern Europe is a lot like a day at the auto races. If you can get around the track in one piece, winning will take care of itself.

That's what we do at Willard.

Postscript

This is a book that could and will go on, though perhaps not on the printed page. I chose a time to stop typing which is a snapshot moment that is arbitrary at best and mercurial at worst.

The book was written over a forced march of 45 days. More than 95 per cent of the contents came strictly from memory. I intended it to be more recollection than a reciting of facts and circumstances. Though written quickly, it simmered and was revised often over the next two years.

In focusing on a latter stanza of my life, I wonder if I short-changed earlier relationships and family that forged who I am. Was I attentive enough to a first wife, who was my rock through nearly 30 years? Are these questions or apologies?

What about the many employees I have had at Willard, those not mentioned but who greatly contributed to the story as valuable stagehands. Olga Golubeva, the finance director who always steered us right, and a deputy finance director, Larisa Yanyuk, who is one of the nicest people on the planet. Sergey Maystrenko, the IT guy who I called Mayo for unknown reasons, a fellow who smiled through turmoil, holding his temper in check when I was unreasonable. Igor Panchenko. Tanya Patokova, Igor Kovriga, Yulia Bayun, Inna Bayeva, Elena Gumenyuk....

All contributed to who we were and what we became. There are others I am sure I have missed – only because I am aged and absent minded. Please just write your name in the space below.

The Man in the Black Cowboy Hat

He was the man with the black cowboy hat, an erudite fellow who could and would debate a point into a black hole and see the truth come out on the other side. He could be cantankerous. I once referred to him as Yosemite Sam, the cartoon character.

H. Glen Willard, age 68, died Dec. 29, 2010 in Kyiv. He was a lawyer's lawyer and an accountant's accountant, though in truth over the last 20 years he practiced those professions in an ad hoc manner, primarily for friends and often, casual acquaintances.

Much of that time he was helping me, for which I am eternally grateful. He was my older brother by nearly three years, my friend, my advisor and my confidante.

A cancerous tumor at the back of his mouth had taken away his voice. In the last months, he carried a notepad and would write down what he wished to say. His weight had dropped to 45 kilo, and his face was drawn. He was frustrated by his illness.

To be sure, though, those final days were some of my best days with Glen. Sitting in the lobby of the Hyatt, because it was a stone's throw from both of our apartments, we reminisced. We traveled country roads in our minds to places familiar.

It was there he wrote on the pad he wanted to be buried at the rural Union Cemetery in North Mississippi, somewhere between William Faulkner's Oxford and New Albany. Willard relatives are buried there, including a grandfather and grandmother.

I don't know what people around Kyiv thought of Glen. I know he had many friends, and that he liked to be around people. He liked good conversation and a good argument, the latter he took for serious mental combat.

He also liked to talk and he liked good food – not the fancy stuff, but collard greens, black-eyed peas and fried okra. After he lost his voice and the ability to eat anything but liquids, he also started to lose his hearing. It frustrated and upset him. Just weeks before his death, he had an operation to restore his hearing.

Glen was often seen with a book, a computer and a knapsack, either at O'Brien's or the Sunduk Pub near Independence Square. A splash of Jim Beam in a Classic Coca-Cola with loads of ice seemed to ease the pain of his tumor.

As for that tumor, it had a war on its hands: Glen suited up for battle and, along with young Dr. Sergey Zemkov, in whom Glen had total confidence, he waged a near- epic struggle for two years. He underwent chemotherapy on several occasions and took massive dosages of radiation.

He lost his hair – twice – and for the longest time his neck was near crimson from radiation burns. The doctor and his patient looked for modern laser surgery around the world, but were turned down by hospitals in London, Miami, Seoul and elsewhere because of the tumor's delicate location.

In the end, Glen admitted some arguments simply can't be won, and was content to be in control of his last days. Other than his wife, Galina, he leaves two children, Stacy and Whitney, both of Atlanta, Ga., and two grandchildren, as well as our mother, Mary Willard, age 89. There are two other siblings, Joy Willard-Williford, an Episcopalian minister, of Melbourne, Fla, and Alan Willard, of Orlando.

Glen was drawn to Ukraine 13 years ago to help me acquire that which would become The Willard Group from the international company Burson-Marsteller and its parent, Young & Rubicam. He was instrumental to our growth to Moscow and Istanbul.

I called on Glen in 1998 because he was the one person I knew I could count on. His wife, Carolyn, had died the previous year, and he was casting about for somewhere to land. He was the person with whom I have always said I would most want to share a foxhole in times of trouble.

Perhaps Glen's greatest role with Willard was as editor of The Ukrainian Observer, a publication that lasted for seven years, much of the time with Glen guiding the editorial content. It was during this time that the magazine was at its colorful best, taking on issues that landed us in hot water but gained the respect of the community.

Shortly after coming to Ukraine, Glen met and fell in love with Galina. She was from Western Ukraine, and they bought an apartment in Bursytn, near L'viv, but Glen commuted often to Kyiv where he also kept an apartment.

Glen was always an overachiever He wrapped up his undergraduate degree at the University of Mississippi in three years while working in the school cafeteria. He obtained his law degree from the University of Tennessee while working 30 to 40 hours a week teaching accounting classes.

On graduating from law school, he formed a law practice in Humboldt, Tennessee, but found small-town law confining. He joined the Arthur Anderson accounting firm in Atlanta, where he quickly became a manager.

For much of his career, he practiced corporate and tax law at Willard & Rushing in Atlanta. In the mid 80s, he merged that firm with Neely & Player. He was admitted to the bar in Georgia and Tennessee.

Glen was an expert at workouts, acquisitions and consolidations, but I guess the best description was that he simply solved other people's problems, whether personal or business. Though at times he had been relatively wealthy, money never motivated him.

He brought a creative spark to nearly every issue. Often, he would dwell on a problem for several days before emerging in a Eureka moment with an innovative solution that brought sides together as it stripped away the subterfuge. It was always a reality-based solution.

I worked closely with Glen for nearly a decade and a half. As associates know, we didn't always get along. We agreed more than we disagreed, but when we disagreed most who really knew us also knew we would reach a compromise by the end of the day.

Glen was the person I counted on when the chips were down. He helped guide me in forming Willard. He was at my side when we engaged in a Herculean battle with the communications conglomerate WPP and Young & Rubicam. In a downturn, he stood shoulder-to-shoulder in helping right the boat.

But he had been there all my life. Long ago, when the board of trustees at what became Orlando University was threatening to kick me out because of my editorials promoting African-American integration of the school, he advised me to carry on.

We withstood that small hurricane and many others together. When I have to make a serious decision from now on, I will ask: "What would Glen advise?"

My Kyiv family at my third art exhibition at Ivan Kavaleridze Museum May 2009. From L to R: My wife Olga, daughter Valya, the artist, Masha and Mia.

My son Rob aka "Life the Guardian" came to visit me in 2005 in Kyiv. A hip-hop performer, he appeared at various night clubs, on television and held a news conference. During rehearsals, we clowned around a little.

It wasn't our intention to be different at our Creative Village, only better. We wanted an atmosphere where creativity was unbridled and individual freedom flourished.

We did away with the nine-to-five workday, and came up with the 24-hour freedom solution – meaning simply get the job done and done well within the span of an entire day and night. In our business, work shouldn't be a forced march.

We encouraged Willard people to work where they felt most productive and creative – at home, in the office, even from a cafe with wireless Internet access.

Along the way, we tore ourselves away from the structure of telephone landlines, going all mobile, all Wi-Fi. We even did away with traditional desks,

giving our team free rein of every floor at our Creative Village. On nice days, we can even work outside.

We realize that the freedom solution might not be for everyone, but if you are in our business – advertising and public relations – it's a winning concept.

So, if you would like to work at Willard's Creative Village, contact Mike.Willard@twg.com.ua.

We are looking for good people.
This recession will not last forever.

Willard

RISK TAKERS. RULE BREAKERS. OPPORTUNITY MAKERS.
KYIV • MOSCOW • ISTANBUL
PHONE +380 50 346 8670

Advertising, Public Relations, Governmental Relations, Strategic Web Development, Publishing

We dubbed our new office the Creative Village and instituted what we called the "Freedom Solution" to work, with an open office, liberal working hours instead of the traditional 9 to 6 and mobile office concept.

When the going gets tough, the tough get going. We became pirates when an international conglomerate attempted to put us out of business. But, good pirates.

In his 90th year, I visited my old boss, Sen. Robert Byrd, in his Senate Appropriations Committee office. I worked for him for eight years when he was Democratic Leader of the Senate. He was my friend and mentor. He died in June 2010. In the picture with Sen. Byrd are Olga, Valya and me.

Harold Burson, chairman emeritus and founder of Bursom-Marsteller, visited Willard's Moscow office in 2005 and posed for a picture with staff.

Other Books by J. Michael Willard

The Flak: A PR Journey

The Flak is Mike Willard's personal journey into the world of public relations. Taking an autobiographical approach and drawing upon his experience, he writes about the importance of creativity, straight talk, and unfettered counsel in the public relations industry. Willard weaves his personal story of successes, defeats, and comebacks into a book loaded with PR know-how gathered by more than a quarter century in the business.

Publ. Price: $30.00
Hardcover, 393 pages
ISBN: 978-966-7889-01-2
– English-language edition;
ISBN: 978-966-7889-05-0
– Russian-language edition.

The Accidental Headline

Mike Willard draws on his 30-plus years' experience as a reporter, editor, government communications and international public relations executive to teach how to get your messages into print and on the air. Explode the "spin" myth and focus on solving problems and communicating key messages.

by J. Michael Willard

Publ. Price: $20.00
Paperback, 143 pages
ISBN: 978-966-96034-0-1

Dancing with the Bear: Crisis Management in Eastern Europe

Bad things do happen to good people and good companies, and they happen twice as often in the countries of the former Soviet Union. In Dancing with the Bear, Mike Willard dispenses practical advice given the realities of risky markets, and recommends ways to help identify and manage various types of crises.

Publ. Price: $22.00
Paperback, 142 pages
ISBN: 978-966-95608-5-8

The Portfolio Bubble: Surviving Professionally at 60

A guide for professionals who don't aspire to retire! At 50 you have a good salary, a nameplate on the door that reads "Senior VP" and even a marked parking place close to the building. You, my friend, are an accident waiting to happen. You are a clay pigeon just out of the chute, and are in the sights of a double-barreled shotgun in the hands of a 35-year-old. You are approaching that vulnerable period called the Portfolio Bubble. Ensuring your career's survival requires that you prepare now.

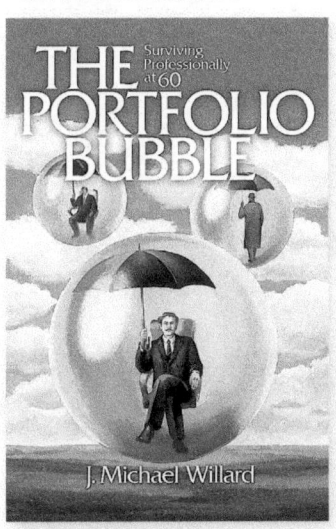

Publ. Price: $25.00
Paperback, 196 pages
ISBN-13: 978-966-96034-1-8
ISBN-10: 966-96034-1-2
Library of Congress Control Number: 2005922396

www.ingramcontent.com/pod-product-compliance
Lightning Source LLC
Chambersburg PA
CBHW050203230526
45470CB00001B/212